Minnesota

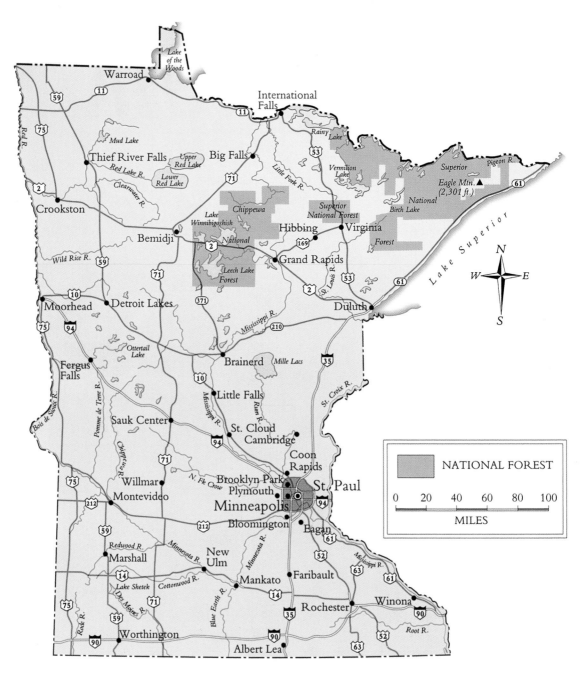

MINNESOTA BY ROAD

Lake of the Woods

Warroad

International Falls

Rainy Lake

Mud Lake

Thief River Falls

Upper Red Lake

Big Falls

Red Lake R.

Lower Red Lake

Vermilion Lake

Superior

Eagle Mtn. (2,301 ft.)

Pigeon R.

Crookston

Clearwater R.

Chippewa

Superior National Forest

National Birch Lake

Bemidji

Lake Winnibigoshish

Hibbing

Virginia

Forest

Wild Rice R.

National

Grand Rapids

Leech Lake Forest

St. Louis R.

Lake Superior

Moorhead

Detroit Lakes

Duluth

N

W   E

S

Ottertail Lake

Mississippi R.

Fergus Falls

Brainerd

Mille Lacs

Bois de Sioux R.

Pomme de Terre R.

Little Falls

Rum R.

St. Croix R.

Sauk Center

Mississippi R.

St. Cloud

Cambridge

NATIONAL FOREST

Chippewa R.

Willmar

N. Fk. Crow

Coon Rapids

0   20   40   60   80   100

Brooklyn Park

Plymouth

St. Paul

MILES

Montevideo

Minneapolis

Bloomington

Eagan

Redwood R.

Minnesota R.

New Ulm

Mississippi R.

Marshall

Mississippi R.

Faribault

Lake Shetek

Cottonwood R.

Mankato

Winona

Des Moines R.

Blue Earth R.

Rochester

Root R.

Rock R.

Worthington

Albert Lea

Celebrate the States

Minnesota

Martin Schwabacher and Patricia K. Kummer

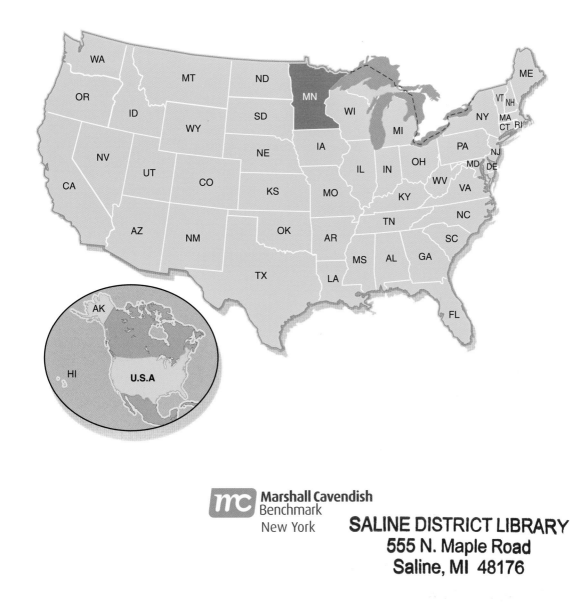

Marshall Cavendish
Benchmark
New York

Marshall Cavendish Benchmark
99 White Plains Road
Tarrytown, NY 10591-9001
www.marshallcavendish.us

All Internet addresses were correct and accurate at the time of printing.

Library of Congress Cataloging-in-Publication Data
Schwabacher, Martin.
Minnesota / by Martin Schwabacher and Patricia K. Kummer. —2nd ed.
p. cm. — (Celebrate the states)
Summary: "Provides comprehensive information on the geography, history, wildlife, governmental
structure, economy, cultural diversity, peoples, religion, and landmarks of
Minnesota"—Provided by publisher.
Includes bibliographical references and index.
ISBN 978-0-7614-2716-2
1. Minnesota—Juvenile literature. I. Kummer, Patricia K. II. Title. III. Series.
F606.3.S39 2008
977.6—dc22
2007002895

Editor: Christine Florie
Publisher: Michelle Bisson
Art Director: Anahid Hamparian
Series Designer: Adam Mietlowski

Photo research by Connie Gardner

Cover photo by Layne Kennedy/CORBIS

The photographs in this book are used by permission and through the courtesy of: *Corbis*: David
Stocklein, back cover; Richard Hamilton Smith, 12, 78; Phil Schemeister, 15, 92, 104; Layne Kennedy,
18, 20, 48, 61, 81, 89, 98, 137; Ed Wargin, 24; David Muench, 28; Minnesota Historical Society, 38,
39, 47; Underwood and Underwood, 43; Owen Franken, 57; Annie Griffiths Belt, 62; Roger Ressmeyer,
86; Corbis, 99; Tom Bean, 102; James L. Amos, 118; Bettmann, 124, 126, 129; CinemaPhoto, 127;
Mitchell Gerber, 131; *North Wind Picture Agency*: 32; *The Granger Collection*: 33,34,36; *AP Photo*:
Lincoln Journal Star/Ken Blackbird, 52; Jim Mone, 68; Bob Rossiter, 71; *PhotoEdit*: Skjold Photoraphs,
55; Cleo Photography, 76; *Superstock*: Richard Cummins, 95; *Dembinsky Photo Associates*: Jason Lindsey,
3; Bill Lea, 19; John Pennoyer, 109 (B); Mark Thomas, 113; *Alamy*: Jason Lindsey, 11; Steve Skjold, 72,
90, 119; Andre Jenny, 134; *Getty*: Michael S. Quinton/National Geographic, 109 (T); Peter
Essick/Aurora, 59; Tom Bean, 13; Hulton Archive, 31, 37; Paul Chesley/Stone, 97; Bill Alkofer, 105;
The Image Works: Sjkold, 16, 50, 56; Frozen Images, 21; Michael Siluk, 63,82,94; Andre Jenny, 66;
Eastcott-Momatiuk, 74; *Art Resource*: Smithsonian American Art Museum, Washington DC, 26;
HIP/Art Resource, NY, 30; Bob King, 83.

Printed in Malaysia
1 3 5 6 4 2

Contents

Minnesota Is . . .

A land of lakes . . .

"Our summer home evokes thoughts of red sunsets, pristine forests, superb fishing, the mournful song of the loons, eagles soaring above, waterskiing, boat rides, jumping in the lake, and most importantly—a perfectly peaceful retreat where all the family loves to be."

—Kent and Elaine Wilson, Lake Vermilion

. . . and of year-round outdoor activities.

"I like swimming when it's hot. I like when it is Christmas and it snows, but I don't like slipping and falling on my butt!"

—Sadie, three and one-half years old

"Run, run, run—the Twin Cities Marathon and Grandma's Marathon in Duluth are two of the most beautiful in the country."

—Earl McDowell, marathon runner from Bloomington

A state of cities with a small-town feel . . .

"I live in downtown Mankato with my husband who has lived here all his life and seems to know everyone. I enjoy that comfort. I also enjoy the empty streets on Sunday mornings!"

—Betty Widmer Blace, Mankato

. . . and of people who care for one another.

"The Minnesota spirit of compassion is revealed in the number of volunteers who help those in need through working at food shelves, delivering meals, providing transportation, repairing homes, and donating funds."

—Carlene McDowell, VEAP volunteer

A state that values education . . .

"For years, Minnesotans have made education a top priority . . . and the results have paid off. From 1980–2002, Minnesota ranked number 1 in the U.S. in education."
   —Christy Mulligan, Teen Central Librarian, Minneapolis Public Library

. . . and culture.
"Minnesota remains such a fantastic place to live because of our rich heritage of community-based arts organizations, artists, and organizers."
                              —Reggie Prim, Community Programs Manager,
                                            Walker Art Center, Minneapolis

"Minnesotans, in every county and city of the state, care about the arts. They understand how valuable the arts are in their own lives, their children's lives, and in the lives of their communities."
                              —James A. Dusso, interim executive director,
                                            Minnesota State Arts Board

"From the exciting Guthrie in downtown Minneapolis to charming playhouses on main streets across the state, Minnesota proves again and again that theater is for everyone."
                              —Beth Burns, Guthrie Theater

Minnesota is best known as the Land of 10,000 Lakes and for its long, cold winters. Yet Minnesota is so much more. In spite of the short growing season, this far-northern state is one of the nation's most productive agricultural areas. Minnesota's rich farmland; thick, shady forests; and deep iron ore mines have provided jobs and incomes for the state's workers. Besides being hard workers, Minnesotans are known as polite, wholesome, healthy, and well-educated people. No wonder Minnesota ranks annually as the best or second-best state in which to live.

Chapter One

The North Star State

One of Minnesota's nicknames is "The North Star State" because the part of Minnesota that juts north into Canada looks like the point of a star. Before Alaska entered the Union in 1959, Minnesota was the northernmost state. The state's northern location helps determine its harsh winter climate, its shady forests, and the kinds of fish, birds, and mammals that make their homes in Minnesota.

Minnesota is in the U.S. subregion called the Upper Midwest. Other Upper Midwest states are Minnesota's neighbors: Wisconsin lies to the east; Iowa, to the south; and North Dakota and South Dakota, to the west. The Canadian provinces of Ontario and Manitoba form Minnesota's northern boundary. Lake Superior's western shore makes up Minnesota's northeastern border.

LAND OF 10,000 LAKES

Minnesota is also known as the Land of 10,000 Lakes, and this is no exaggeration. In fact, Minnesota has more than 14,000 lakes of 10 acres or more, and if smaller ones are counted, the number soars past 15,000.

The Boundary Waters Canoe Area Wilderness was carved by huge glaciers, forming an area more than 1.3 million acres in size.

The state has so many lakes that some have the same name. Minnesota has 201 Mud Lakes, 154 Long Lakes, and 123 Rice Lakes. Sixty-five towns in Minnesota have the word *lake* in their name, not counting words that mean "lake" or "water" in Native-American languages. *Minnesota* itself means "sky-tinted water" in the Dakota language, which is where another of Minnesota's nicknames, "Land of Sky-Blue Waters," comes from.

Most of Minnesota's lakes were formed thousands of years ago, when glaciers inched their way down from the frozen north. These glaciers—some more than a mile thick—gouged deep into the earth, scraping off the soil down to bare bedrock. By the time the glaciers retreated, they had transformed northern Minnesota into a rough, rocky landscape. Melting ice filled in the low spots, creating lakes.

Minnesota's northeastern corner is a triangle shaped like an arrowhead, with the beautiful, rugged north shore of Lake Superior on one side and the Canadian border on the other. The Arrowhead region in between contains thousands of small lakes. In the tranquil Boundary Waters Canoe Area Wilderness, people can canoe for days without seeing another human being or hearing the sound of a motor. Vacationers, such as Tim Starr, come to enjoy "the complete stillness, where the flat water reflects everything you see."

Early fur traders canoed from lake to lake, following rivers or simply carrying their canoes overland to the next lake. The route traced by these hearty travelers from Lake Superior to Lake of the Woods forms part of the state's northern boundary. An odd chunk of land on the northwestern side of Lake of the Woods was included in the United States. This part of Minnesota cannot be reached by land without leaving the United States. It is this section of the state that pokes the farthest north.

There are more than 1,200 miles of canoe routes in the Boundary Waters Canoe Area Wilderness.

In western Minnesota the glaciers had a very different effect. There, when the ice melted, the water created a vast inland sea called Lake Agassiz. This lake existed for thousands of years and was the largest lake on the continent. Over the years, mud and silt settled on the lake bottom. When the giant lake finally drained away, it left behind some of the flattest, richest farmland in North America. This area is called the Red River valley. The wide, flat valley barely rises at all for miles on either side of the Red River, making floods particularly devastating. Locals successfully fought off floodwater many times over the years, but in 1997 they were hit by the worst flood they had ever seen. "You just can't imagine 50 miles of water around you in every direction," said Jack Thompson of Breckenridge.

The Red River winds through the fertile farmland of western Minnesota.

Wendy Pearson of the National Weather Service said, "You've got to have a lot of respect for the water. What it can do is awesome."

A wide swath of lakes curves up the middle of Minnesota. These lakes formed between the mounds of dirt and crushed rock left behind by the glaciers. This lake region marks the eastern edge of the Great Plains, which sweep uninterrupted over the bottom of the state. Rippling grassland once stretched as far as the eye could see. In the 1800s the painter George Catlin said that the horizon formed "a perfect straight line around us, like that of the blue and boundless ocean." Today, the prairie has been fenced off into neat farms. A layer of rich topsoil that was pushed ahead of the glaciers as they surged south gave southern Minnesota some of the country's most fertile farmland.

IN LOVE WITH THE PRAIRIE

A vast sea of grass once covered much of the United States, including one-third of Minnesota. The endless prairie awed early settlers, who felt tiny in the shoulder-high grasses. Wild prairies contained hundreds of kinds of plants. Today, most prairies have been replaced by farms, where just a few plants are grown at a time.

A growing number of people have fallen in love with the rich but subtle variety of a truly wild prairie. Steve Henke and Nancy Peltola, who own land in southern Minnesota, trade seeds with other prairie lovers to re-create the variety of plants that once grew wild. Wandering through their little patch of prairie, Steve points out his new friends. "This is pussy toes . . . buffalo pea . . . harebell . . . wild rose. . . . Here's one of my favorites, prairie smoke. It looks like a puff of smoke."

A true prairie must burn now and then to keep other plants from moving in. Plains Indians used to set fires regularly to corral game, renew pastures, and drive off insects. Steve and Nancy carefully burned 12 acres of their prairie to help restore it to the way it once was. "Two weeks later," Steve said, "you couldn't tell it had ever been burned."

LAND AND WATER

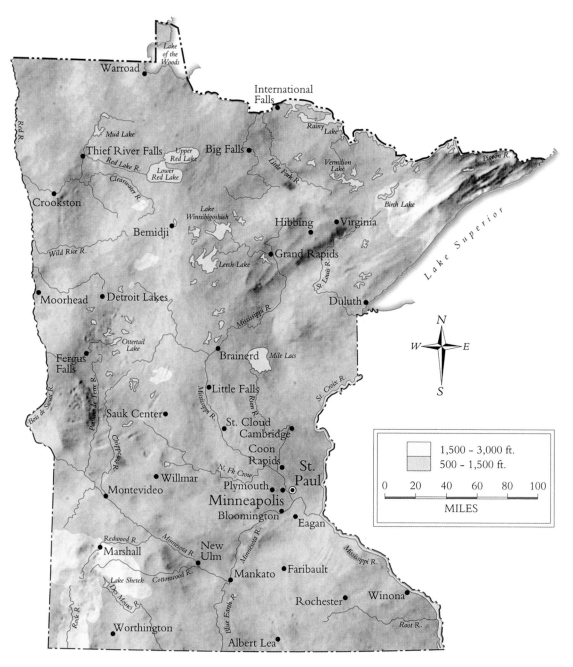

Warroad

Lake of the Woods

International Falls

Rainy Lake

Red R.

Mud Lake

Thief River Falls

Upper Red Lake

Big Falls

Little Fork R.

Vermilion Lake

Pigeon R.

Red Lake R.

Lower Red Lake

Clearwater R.

Crookston

Bemidji

Lake Winnibigoshish

Hibbing

Virginia

Birch Lake

Grand Rapids

Lake Superior

Wild Rice R.

Leech Lake

St. Louis R.

Moorhead

Detroit Lakes

Mississippi R.

Duluth

Ottertail Lake

Brainerd

Mile Lacs

Fergus Falls

St. Croix R.

Bois de Sioux R.

Pomme de Terre R.

Little Falls

Sauk Center

Mississippi R.

Rum R.

St. Cloud
Cambridge

Chippewa R.

Coon Rapids

St. Paul

Willmar

N. Fk. Crow

Plymouth

Minneapolis

Montevideo

Bloomington

Eagan

Redwood R.

Minnesota R.

New Ulm

Minnesota R.

Mississippi R.

Marshall

Mankato

Faribault

Lake Shetek

Cottonwood R.

Winona

Des Moines R.

Rochester

Rock R.

Blue Earth R.

Root R.

Worthington

Albert Lea

N
W   E
S

	1,500 – 3,000 ft.
	500 – 1,500 ft.

0   20   40   60   80   100

MILES

The southeastern tip of Minnesota is the only part of the state that the glaciers did not reach. According to the writer D. J. Tice, "The southeast is a lakeless land of cold, rushing streams, high ridges, plunging ravines, and green-brown valleys rolling lazily into the distance, soft and lumpy as featherbeds." Though this area has almost no lakes, it's still a great place to fish, with some of the best fly-fishing streams anywhere.

Minnesota has 15,000 miles of rivers, including the Red River of the North and the Bois de Sioux, which form parts of the state's western border, and the St. Croix and the Mississippi, which form parts of the eastern border. The Minnesota River joins the Mississippi at St. Paul, the state capital. The mighty Mississippi, the nation's most important river, starts in northern Minnesota as a tiny stream trickling out of Lake Itasca. When all of Minnesota's lakes, rivers, streams, and ponds are added together, they equal 4,059 square miles of water.

In Itasca State Park, visitors can wade in the shallow waters of the Mississippi River headwaters.

COLD, HOT, AND IN BETWEEN

Minnesota is famous for frigid weather, and deservedly so. The cold winters force Minnesotans to put on so much clothing, they sometimes look like puffy marshmallows. The temperature falls below 0 degrees Fahrenheit an average of thirty-four days each year in the Twin Cities and sixty-eight days in International Falls, way up north near the Canadian border. International Falls often records the coldest temperature anywhere in the Lower 48 states—it's not uncommon to see the thermometer dip to −40° F there. During a record cold snap in 1996, when the town reached −60° F, every school in the state was closed.

Except for the very coldest times, however, kids have a great time in the snow. They go sledding, build snowmen and forts, and have snowball fights.

Young Minnesotans enjoy the state's cold, snowy weather.

"I love Minnesota winters," said Minnesota native Dan Barton. "Everything is clear. Powdery snow is everywhere—the world is new. The entire neighborhood turns into a playground."

Of course, winter in Minnesota is not all fun and games. Darkness comes early in winter, and for some people it's just too cold to go outside if they can help it. "When it gets to be six to nine months, it gets to be a lot," one Minnesotan admitted. "You go to school or work in the morning, it's dark and cold. You get out in the evening, it's dark and cold. You get cabin fever."

While Minnesota's winters are famous, fewer people know that Minnesota's summers can also be uncomfortable. There are many lovely days, but July and August can be hot and muggy, with temperatures occasionally breaking 100° F. And Minnesota's abundant water creates a perfect breeding ground for mosquitoes. In remote areas, campers wear nets to protect themselves from swarming insects. Ken Baldwin, who lives in a swampy, wooded area in central Minnesota, said he has to brush himself off 30 feet from his house, then run to the door so he doesn't bring a cloud of mosquitoes inside with him. "When the sun's out and there's a little bit of a breeze, it doesn't bother me. But when it's dark in the woods, it can get pretty bad," he said. Many Minnesotans and visitors jokingly say that the mosquito should be the state bird.

Minnesota also experiences spring and fall. Although Minnesota springs are usually only a few weeks between winter and summer, they do bring needed rain for flowers and farm crops. Sometimes the rain is accompanied by severe thunderstorms or damaging tornadoes. Many Minnesotans consider fall to be the state's best season, with lots of sunshine, little rain, and no snow or mosquitoes. The fall colors of Minnesota's leafy trees provide splashes of red, orange, yellow, and brown along city streets and country roads.

A bicyclist enjoys Minnesota's fall foliage.

FORESTS, GRASSES, AND ANIMALS

Three U.S. vegetation zones meet in Minnesota—coniferous forest, deciduous forest, and prairie grassland. The coniferous forest in the northeast covers about 40 percent of the state. Trees in this kind of forest are mainly evergreens: trees with needles and pine cones. Minnesota's conifers include fir, spruce, and red, white, and jack pines. Minnesota's state tree, the Norway pine, is a red pine. Animals in these woods can snack on wild blueberries, raspberries, and blackberries. About 27,000 black bears, 8,000 moose, and 2,600 gray wolves call the pine forest home. Bobcats, lynx, and a few mountain lions roam the area, too. Several kinds of owls and hawks nest in the pine trees.

Minnesota's black bears feast on the wild berries in the state's forests.

Minnesota's deciduous forest starts in the state's southeast corner and then runs north in a narrow band along the western edge of the coniferous forest. Deciduous trees drop their leaves in the fall. The main leaf-bearing trees in this part of Minnesota are aspen, basswood, birch, butternut, elm, hickory, maple, and oak. In the spring and summer colorful wildflowers sprout up. Among them are anemones, asters, bellworts, Dutchman's britches, goldenrod, hepaticas, trillium, and woodland sunflowers. However, some forest plants are fading away. For example, the dwarf trout lily is an endangered species, and American ginseng is at risk.

Prairie grassland covers southwestern Minnesota and continues north in a narrow band along the western deciduous forest. About one thousand kinds of grasses grow in the prairie's rich soil, including bluestem, Indian grass, and porcupine grass. Wildflowers such as golden Alexanders, lady's slippers, pasqueflowers, purple and white clovers, and purple coneflowers add color to the grasslands. Among these flowers are two threatened species—prairie bush clover and the western prairie fringed orchid. In a few places, groups of bur oak trees stand out. Bobolinks, Savannah sparrows, and western meadowlarks are a few prairie birds. Game birds of the prairie include partridges, sharp-tailed grouse, and ring-necked pheasants.

Sharp-tailed grouse partake in their ritual mating dance in Minnesota's prairie.

Altogether, Minnesota has more than four hundred kinds of birds. Many of them only stop for a while as they fly north or south along the Mississippi flyway. Minnesota's state bird, the common loon, can often be seen on northern lakes. A black-and-white bird noted for its red eyes and white necklace, the loon is much loved for its distinctive call, which sounds like eerie, ghostly laughter. Other waterbirds include

Minnesota's state bird is the common loon.

black-crowned night herons, Canada geese, double-crested cormorants, great blue herons, and great egrets. At one time burrowing owls nested in the prairie. This owl is no longer native to Minnesota. The bald eagle, greater prairie chicken, osprey, and sandhill crane almost disappeared in Minnesota, too. Several state projects restored their habitats and helped bring them back. Currently, the bald eagle and the northern Great Plains piping plover are threatened species, and the Great Lakes piping plover is an endangered species in Minnesota.

Of Minnesota's 157 kinds of fish, game fish such as northern pike, largemouth bass, brook trout, bluegills, and walleye pike are the best known. Minnesota's largest fish are lake sturgeon and flathead catfish—both of which can weigh more than 100 pounds.

Many other animals are found throughout the state. The most commonly seen ones are chipmunks, cottontail rabbits, raccoons, squirrels, and white-tailed deer. Gray wolves, also called timber wolves, are more likely heard than seen. Although wolves do not attack people, their howls send shivers up people's spines. Minnesota is the only state besides Alaska in which gray wolves were never completely wiped out. In 1974 wolves were protected under the Endangered Species Act. Bill Berg of the Minnesota Department of Natural Resources said, "People have come to accept the wolf as a critter they can live with." The efforts to save the wolf have been so successful that wolves now roam across almost half the state. The gray wolf is no longer on the endangered species list.

PROTECTING THE ENVIRONMENT

Minnesotans love the outdoors, but sometimes they disagree over how best to enjoy their state's natural beauty. One argument arose over the use of Jet Skis, which allow people to zoom around on the water.

Though Jet Skis are exciting to ride, they can be a nuisance. Instead of listening to the gentle lapping of the waves, everyone at the lake must listen to the constant buzzing of a motor. "People are saying, 'Give us some relief,'" said the state representative Kris Hasskamp. "We're asking for four hours in a day to have some peace to listen to the loons." Many people wanted to ban the machines completely from smaller lakes, while others fought any restrictions. In 1997 the state legislature passed a law that limited the use of Jet Skis to daytime hours, from 9:30 A.M. to one hour before sunset. Now everyone can enjoy the setting sun in silence.

Disputes also arise over the use of snowmobiles. The pristine Boundary Waters Canoe Area Wilderness bans them, but Voyageurs National Park allows them in certain areas. Some argue that with thousands of miles of snowmobile trails elsewhere in the state, parks such as Voyageurs should be left in serene, natural silence. Others contend that snowmobiles allow people to go places in winter they could not reach otherwise. David Dill, a frequent visitor to Voyageurs, respects both views. "When I take people snowmobiling here, I just love to stop and turn the lights off. Their eyes start to adjust, and they say, 'Oh my God!' and they see the sky is just a mass of stars. And the wolves start calling, and it's just this incredible environmental experience."

Besides the noise pollution that Jet Skis and snowmobiles make, the fuels they use also contribute to air and water pollution. Protecting the water in Minnesota's lakes, rivers, and wetlands is an important job for the state's government and people. As Governor Tim Pawlenty stated, "More so than any other state, the quality and quantity of water in Minnesota is central to our way of life. It helps define who we are and what we value." In 2006 the state legislature passed the Clean Water Legacy Act to protect and clean up the state's water surfaces.

Minnesota's snowmobiling enthusiasts have to obey rules and regulations to protect the natural environment in which they ride.

This act also provided measures to rebuild riverbanks to prevent flooding and to reinforce lakeshores to prevent unsafe runoff from entering the water.

While Minnesotans work hard to protect endangered and threatened plants and animals, they work just as hard to prevent alien plants and animals from harming the environment. Zebra mussels and Eurasian water milfoil are the main culprits. Zebra mussels are European shellfish that entered the Great Lakes on ships from Europe. These mussels attach themselves to ships, small boats, and other shellfish and clog water pipes. From Lake Superior the zebra mussel has spread to Minnesota's lakes and rivers, where they eat the food of native mussels and therefore crowd them out. The Eurasian water milfoil is a feathery plant that also hitched rides on ships from Europe and Asia and spread to Minnesota's lakes. These milfoils grow rapidly and shade out native water plants, preventing them from growing. Minnesotans prevent the spread of these alien invaders from lake to lake by washing their boats, propellers, and fishing gear before using them in another lake or river.

Chapter Two

From Ancient Times to the Twenty-First Century

About 12,000 years ago the first people, known as Paleo-Indians, had reached Minnesota. These people are also often called the Clovis people or Big Game Hunters. As the last glaciers in what is now Minnesota were melting, the Paleo-Indians followed huge animals south. These people hunted mammoths, which looked like huge elephants, and giant bison that were twice the size of today's buffalo. As the climate grew warmer, the huge animals died out, and the Paleo-Indians began to settle in more permanent campsites. They learned to pick berries and nuts and to catch fish. They also hunted smaller game, such as white-tailed deer, rabbits, beaver, and muskrats. The Paleo-Indians were the ancestors of today's Native Americans.

EARLY NATIVE AMERICANS

Around seven thousand years ago early Native Americans were living throughout what is now Minnesota. Near Lake Superior these early people

George Caitlin illustrates a Sioux village on the plains of early Minnesota.

pounded chunks of copper into knife blades, spear points, and jewelry. Archaeologists believe these were the first people in North America to make tools from copper. At the same time people on Minnesota's prairie had tamed dogs, were hunting buffalo, and had learned how to grind grain by hand. In both the forests and prairies these early people wove baskets and made pottery containers.

About five thousand years ago early people in southern Minnesota made petroglyphs, or pictures carved into rocks. Some of these carvings show people carrying spears. Also in southern Minnesota, Native Americans

Early Native Americans made carvings in rocks that showed important events, ceremonies, animals, and hunting.

carved soft red stone called caitlinite—now known as pipestone—into peace pipes decorated with religious symbols.

Native Americans throughout the Upper Midwest had begun burying their dead in huge burial mounds about 2,500 years ago. At one time more than ten thousand mounds stood in Minnesota. Only a few of them remain today. One of them, Grand Mound in northern Minnesota, contains 5,000 tons of earth and might have held about 5,500 bodies.

By one thousand years ago early people in what is now southern Minnesota lived in towns, hunted with bows and arrows, caught fish with hooks and lines, and made beautifully decorated clay pots. Throughout Minnesota people had begun gathering the grass known as wild rice and were planting corn, beans, and squash.

THE DAKOTA AND OJIBWE PEOPLE

By the 1500s Minnesota's Native Americans were called the Santee Sioux, one of the groups of Dakota people. They moved from place to place, following the cycle of the seasons. In the spring they collected sap from maple trees to make sugar. They also fished, hunted ducks and geese, and caught muskrats and beavers for their warm fur. When the weather grew warmer, they planted corn and other vegetables. During the summer the Santee lived in large wooden buildings that each housed two or three families. The women collected berries and roots, and the men hunted buffalo. As summer ended, they harvested the corn, drying as much as they could for the winter. In the fall they traveled to the lakes and swamps to collect wild rice. When the weather grew cold, they moved into the forests and put up snug tents called tepees. During the long winter months they hunted, ate the food they had stored, and sang songs and told stories.

Santee Sioux men hunt buffalo.

In the late 1600s the Ojibwe people, a Native-American group from Wisconsin and southern Canada, had moved into northern Minnesota. The Ojibwe were also known as the Chippewa or Anishinabe, meaning "the first people." They had moved west in search of new fur-trapping lands. The Ojibwe traded their furs with the French, who had arrived in North America during the early 1600s. For winter hunting and trapping the Ojibwe made snowshoes that allowed them to walk easily on top of the snow. In warmer weather the Ojibwe built and paddled lightweight birchbark canoes that carried them along the trade routes of Minnesota's lakes and rivers. Eventually, the Ojibwe began hunting and fishing on land used by the Santee, which led to several conflicts. By 1750 the Ojibwe had gained control of northern Minnesota. The Santee were pushed south onto Minnesota's grasslands. Today, the location of Ojibwe reservations and Santee communities remain in those same areas of Minnesota.

Ojibwe tribe members repair their canoe with bark.

THE FUR TRADE

In 1660 a Frenchman named Pierre Radisson visited Minnesota. He wrote about the great opportunities to trade for furs with the Indians. Soon French and English traders were making the long journey to Minnesota. The English came from Hudson Bay, far to the north. The French came in canoes following the St. Lawrence River and the chain of Great Lakes.

The hardy French fur traders were called voyageurs. They got up at 4 or 5 A.M. and paddled until dark, not eating dinner until 9 or 10 P.M. They could travel almost anywhere in northern Minnesota by carrying their canoes from one lake to the next. These tiring walks were called portages. Even though the voyageurs' canoes were sometimes 45 feet long, carrying them was not the hard part—their cargo weighed much more than the canoes. The bundles of furs weighed up to 80 pounds each, and the men often carried two at a time. It was a rugged, exhausting life, but it was not without its pleasures for those who liked the wild outdoors.

By the 1700s British traders were competing with the French for control of the fur trade. This led to the French and Indian War (1756–1763). In Minnesota the Ojibwe helped the French, and the Santee Sioux aided the British. France lost that war, and Britain gained France's land in Canada and east of the Mississippi River.

Rough and rugged fur traders traveled by land and by water to collect as many pelts as they could.

BECOMING A STATE

For about twenty years Minnesota east of the Mississippi belonged to Great Britain. When the American colonies won their independence from Britain in 1783, Minnesota east of the Mississippi became part of the Northwest Territory of the United States. In 1803 the United States doubled in size by buying a vast tract of land west of the Mississippi from France in a transaction called the Louisiana Purchase. At that time the rest of Minnesota became part of the young nation's Louisiana Territory.

In 1820 construction began on a fort where the Minnesota River joins the Mississippi. Fort Snelling housed the area's first school, hospital, library, and post office. The fort was an outpost surrounded by wilderness—the

Fort Snelling served as a defensive barrier for the frontier.

nearest town was 300 miles away. In winter, when the rivers froze, no boats could reach the fort. Sometimes mail got through by dogsled, but in bad weather the people at the fort were completely cut off. In 1826 they received no mail for five months.

Two important settlements were started near Fort Snelling. Just to the north gushed the lovely St. Anthony Falls, the only waterfall on the entire Mississippi River. American settlers used the rushing water to power sawmills and flour mills. The falls eventually became the center of a booming community called St. Anthony, which later became the city of Minneapolis.

Downriver from Fort Snelling was a community called Pig's Eye Landing, named after a saloon keeper there. Pig's Eye Landing was the last place a steamboat traveling upriver could safely reach; after that the water was too shallow. Steamboats eventually became the area's most important

St. Anthony Falls, Minnesota, was the future site of the city of Minneapolis.

connection with the outside world. Whenever a steamboat docked, crowds gathered to greet the arrivals and hear the latest news. Pig's Eye Landing grew into the city of St. Paul.

Gradually, white Americans realized that Minnesota offered more than just furs. It also had plenty of forests that could be logged and fertile land that could be farmed. In 1837 the U.S. government pressured the Santee Sioux into giving up a big chunk of land between the Mississippi and St. Croix rivers. In the next twenty years the United States took control of most of the rest of the Native-American land in the region. In 1849 the U.S. Congress created the Minnesota Territory, which was the first step to statehood.

Minnesota grew rapidly during the 1850s. The territory's white population stood at six thousand in 1850. By 1858, when Minnesota became a state, 150,000 people lived there. In 1854 the first commercial flour mill opened at St. Anthony Falls. By 1858 dozens of mills were harnessing the power of Minnesota's rivers, and by 1870 more than five hundred mills dotted the state. A decade later Minneapolis was the world's major flour-milling city. Pillsbury and Washburn Crosby were the best-known milling companies. Later in the 1900s Washburn Crosby and several smaller companies were brought together and renamed General Mills.

THE CIVIL WAR AND THE DAKOTA WAR

When the conflict between Northern and Southern states over slavery led to the Civil War in April 1861, the Minnesota governor Alexander Ramsey happened to be in Washington, D.C. He quickly offered one thousand men, making Minnesota the first state to volunteer troops for the Union cause. During the war 24,000 Minnesotans went south to fight. One-tenth of them died.

While the country's attention was focused on Civil War battles in the South, fighting broke out back in Minnesota between white settlers and Native Americans. The Santee Sioux had been forced onto reservations along the Minnesota River that were not good for hunting. To survive, they depended on money and food that the U.S. government had promised them in exchange for their land. But little of the food or money was ever delivered, and by 1862 many Santee were starving.

The Santee believed that with so many soldiers fighting the Civil War, they might be able to take back their land. A Santee Sioux chief named Taoyateduta, or Little Crow, urged them to make peace. He realized they had no chance of defeating the U.S. government. "You may kill one—two—ten; yes as many as the leaves in the forest. . . . Kill one—two—ten, and ten times ten will come to kill you," he told them. When his people decided to fight anyway, he said, "I am not a coward. I will die with you."

Bands of Santee Sioux went from farm to farm along the Minnesota River, burning buildings and killing entire families. The former Minnesota governor Henry Sibley, who had traded and lived with the Santee, led a group of soldiers that quickly crushed the rebellion. "We have inflicted so severe a blow upon the red devils that they will not dare to make another stand," he wrote to his wife.

Little Crow was a Sioux chief who reluctantly led his people to an uprising against the U.S. government.

An artist's depiction of Santee Sioux raiding farms during their uprising in 1862.

The captive Santee were brought to trial, and 303 of them were sentenced to death. President Abraham Lincoln ordered most of them freed, but thirty-eight Santee were hanged in Mankato on December 26, 1862, in one of the largest mass executions in U.S. history.

After the Santee uprising, life became much harder for all Native Americans in Minnesota. The Santee reservation along the Minnesota River was taken away, and most Santee people were sent to South Dakota, where many died of hunger and disease. Today, the Ojibwe are the only Native Americans in Minnesota with large reservations. The Santee, meanwhile, have four small reservations in southern Minnesota.

HOMESTEADERS

The vast lands the government had obtained from the Native Americans were soon opened to settlers. But farmers needed railroads to bring their goods to market. To encourage the construction of the railroads, the government gave huge tracts of land to railroad companies—in fact, one-fifth of all the land in Minnesota. The railroads then resold much of the land to farmers and developers, thereby attracting more people to the state.

Newspapers urged people to come to Minnesota and build new lives. In 1854 a *North-Western Democrat* article said, "Come on then; there is plenty of room—good prairie, good timber, good water and everything that an industrious and reasonable man could consider valuable, here awaits the careworn stranger from other parts of the world."

The Homestead Act of 1862 made it possible for pioneering settlers to get 160 acres of land for free from the U.S. government. This enabled poor immigrants from Europe to own land in America. Settlers claimed 1.25 million acres of land in Minnesota between 1863 and 1865. Many were immigrants from Germany and Ireland. Later, Swedes and Norwegians poured in. By 1880 one-third of Minnesotans were immigrants, and many more had foreign-born parents.

THE SECRETARY OF THE STATE BOARD OF IMMIGRATION
Has recently published the following statement, showing the

COST OF COMING TO MINNESOTA.

Immigrants should procure Tickets and contract for the carriage of Extra Baggage through to their ultimate destination, if possible.

EUROPEAN EMIGRANT RATES OF PASSAGE TO ST. PAUL,
FROM

Berlin	$56 00	Rome, Italy	$68 50
Leipzig	56 30	Naples, Italy	71 50
Dresden	59 70	Paris	54 50
Hanover	54 75	Antwerp	45 50
Bremen or Hamburg	54 00	Madgeburg, Prussia	54 65
Stettin	56 80	Cassel	55 70
Danzig	58 55	Cologne	58 05
Konigsburg, Prussia	59 25	Trier	60 05
Copenhagen	54 00	Basel, Switzerland	51 90
Christiana	54 00	Zurich	53 00
Gothenburg, Sweden	54 00	Frankfort on the Main	51 10
London	54 00	Prague, Bohemia	60 10
Queenstown, Ireland	50 50	Vienna	61 80
Liverpool	50 50	Pesth, Hungary	65 60

(100 lbs. baggage allowed to each.)

AMERICAN RATES.

The following are first-class rates, from which emigrants commonly get reductions of from 33¾ to 50 per cent. They also get reduced rates on baggage. Make a bargain always at the Railway Station nearest your starting point.

TO ST. PAUL, FROM

New York	$37 00	Pittsburg, Pa., steamboat	$28 00
Boston, Mass	43 00	St Louis, Mo., "	8 00
Baltimore, Md	34 25	Omaha, Neb	14 70
Philadelphia	35 00	Sioux City, Ia	10 80
Buffalo, N.Y	28 00	Chicago, Ill	14 00
Cleveland, O	23 25	Milwaukee, Wis	11 35
Cincinnati, O., steamboat	18 00	Davenport, Ia	12 05
Detroit, Mich	22 00	Madison, Wis	10 65
Toronto, Canada	28 00	Des Moines, Ia	11 30
Memphis, Tenn., steamboat	22 10	La Crosse, Wis	5 35
Davenport, Ia., "	6 50	" steamboat	2 75

The local rates within this State are generally four cents per mile, and half fare to immigrants. But special rates are given on all the roads to immigrants for fare and baggage or freight, on application to the agents.

A circular from 1870 advertises the cost of traveling to Minnesota from all over the world.

THE LOGGING BOOM

When white settlers began moving into Minnesota, two-thirds of the state was covered with trees. At the same time, logging companies gained control of timberlands that Native Americans had been forced to give up. Lumberjacks, many of whom were Native Americans, worked for the logging companies. The lumberjacks spent the cold winters cutting trees and dragging logs to the nearest river. When the ice melted, they stamped their company's mark on the logs and sent them floating downstream. Rivers such as the St. Croix sometimes got jammed with thousands of logs. When the logs arrived at mill towns, they were sawed into boards.

After trees were cut and stamped, loggers pushed them in the river to float downstream to the mill.

THE SHANTYMAN'S LIFE

During the Minnesota logging boom, which peaked in the 1890s, thousands of men made their living cutting timber and hauling it out of the woods. Many loggers lived in crude huts called shanties. This song comes from the town of Bemidji.

Oh, a shan - ty - man's life is a wear - i - some
Swing - ing an ax from morn till

life, al - though some think it void of care.
night, in the midst of the for - ests drear.

Ly - ing in the shan - ty

bleak and bare, while the cold storm - y win - try winds

Oh, the cook rises up in the middle of the night, saying "Hurrah, brave boys, it's day!"
Broken slumber ofttimes are passed as the cold winter night whiles away.
Had we rum, wine or beer our spirits to cheer, as the days so lonely do dwine,
Or a glass of any shone while in the woods alone for to cheer up our troubled minds.

But when spring does set in, double hardships begin, when the waters are piercing cold,
And our clothes are all wet, and fingers benumbed, and our pike-poles we scarcely can hold.
Betwixt rocks and shoals there's employment for all, as our well-banded raft we steer.
And the rapids that we run, oh, they seem to us but fun, for we're void of all slavish fear.

Oh, a brave shanty lad is the only lad I love, and I never will deny the same.
My heart doth scorn these conceited farmer boys, who think it a disgraceful name.
They may boast of their farms, but my shanty-boy's charms so far exceeds them all;
Until death doth part he shall enjoy my heart, let his riches be great or small.

The logging companies did not plan for the future; they just cut down all the trees they could, leaving stumps and branches that sometimes burned in terrible fires. But while the logging boom lasted, it provided jobs for thousands and made millionaires of the men who owned the companies. By the 1920s, when the logging boom was ending, one-third of the state had been cleared of trees.

MINING

Stretching across northeastern Minnesota is a 100-mile-long ridge that the Ojibwe called Mesabi, or Giant. A lumberman named Lewis Merritt was certain the Mesabi was filled with iron ore. He died in 1880 without finding any iron, but his seven sons kept searching. Although a mine opened in the nearby Vermilion Range in 1884, prospectors in the Mesabi found nothing but a lot of red dirt. Finally, in 1890 one of the Merritts' men had the dirt tested. It was two-thirds iron. Leonidas Merritt marveled, "If we had gotten mad and kicked the ground right where we stood, we would have thrown out 64-percent ore."

The Mesabi Range turned out to be the richest source of iron ore in the entire United States. In most of the country deep mines had to be dug to reach the precious ore. In the Mesabi the glaciers had already done most of the work. The ice floes had scraped off so much rock that in some places the iron lay right on the surface. By 1892 thousands of iron prospectors swarmed over the Mesabi. In 1893 Frank Hibbing led a group of men into the forest in search of iron. One cold January morning Hibbing woke up and said, "My bones feel rusty. I believe there's iron under me." His bones were right, and a mining town called Hibbing soon sprang up on the spot.

Building miles of railroad tracks and fleets of ships to carry tons of ore to the steel mills in Pennsylvania required millions of dollars. East Coast millionaires such as John D. Rockefeller and Andrew Carnegie quickly seized control of the iron industry in Minnesota. When the Merritts fell short of money in 1893, they lost their mining company to Rockefeller.

Open-pit iron mining was performed at this mine in Hibbing.

The big mining companies recruited laborers from Europe, and towns like Hibbing filled with people born in Finland, Italy, Croatia, and many other countries. The mining companies often owned the stores the miners shopped in and even the houses they lived in. When the miners tried to form unions, the companies sometimes hired thugs to beat them up. During a 1907 strike a Finnish-American miner wrote to his brother, "There are 100 stooges with guns paid by the mining companies harassing the workers just like some animals."

Many miners were socialists who thought the riches the mine owners were amassing should be shared with the workers. Polly Bullard, a young schoolteacher on the Iron Range, wrote in 1908 that her landlady was "a rabid Socialist and all the Socialists who come here to speak stay at her house. One came Saturday night and they had a grand to-do down in the kitchen till two in the morning." As the miners married and started families, they demanded that their towns become more than just a jumble of temporary shacks. Led by Victor Power, the "Fighting Mayor" of Hibbing, mining towns were able to provide services such as streetlights, schools, and hospitals by taxing the companies that were making millions of dollars from Minnesota's iron ore.

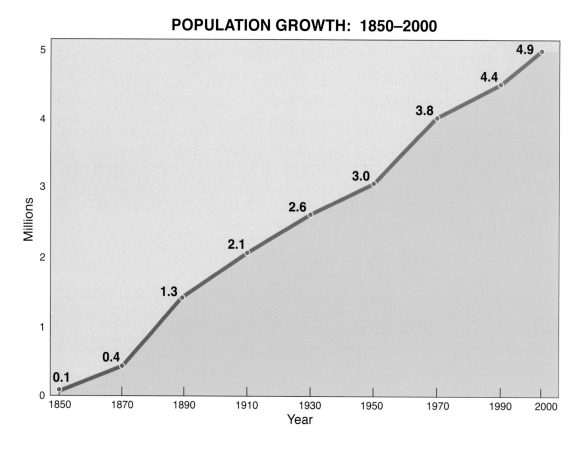

POPULATION GROWTH: 1850–2000

Millions (y-axis)

Year (x-axis)

Data points:
- 1850: 0.1
- 1870: 0.4
- 1890: 1.3
- 1910: 2.1
- 1930: 2.6
- 1950: 3.0
- 1970: 3.8
- 1990: 4.4
- 2000: 4.9

THE GRANGE MOVEMENT

Miners were not the only Minnesotans facing hardships. Minnesota farmers worked hard to raise animals and grow crops; all they wanted was a fair price for their efforts. But they needed railroads to transport their products to cities and had no choice but to pay whatever the railroads charged. They were also charged high prices to store their crops in huge towers called grain elevators. The big milling companies that turned their wheat into flour would only buy the wheat at a low price, so farmers had no place to turn. It seemed that no matter how hard the farmers worked, the railroads, elevators, and mills made most of the profits while the farmers struggled to break even.

A CLOUD OF BUGS

Some of the problems Minnesota farmers faced were more bizarre than low prices. For four years beginning in 1873, millions of grasshoppers invaded their fields and ate everything in sight, including clothes hanging out to dry. In her book *On the Banks of Plum Creek* Laura Ingalls Wilder describes how her father was just about to harvest his first wheat crop in Minnesota when the plague descended.

Plunk! Something hit Laura's head and fell to the ground. She looked down and saw the largest grasshopper she had ever seen. Then huge brown grasshoppers were hitting the ground all around her, hitting her head and her face and her arms. They came thudding down like hail.

The cloud was hailing grasshoppers. The cloud was grasshoppers. Their bodies hid the sun and made darkness. Their thin, large wings gleamed and glittered. The rasping whirring of their wings filled the whole air and they hit the ground and the house with the noise of a hailstorm.

Laura tried to beat them off. Their claws clung to her skin and her dress. They looked at her with bulging eyes, turning their heads this way and that. Mary ran screaming into the house. Grasshoppers covered the ground, there was not one bare bit to step on. Laura had to step on grasshoppers and they smashed squirming and slimy under her feet.

The farmers responded by uniting to form big organizations of their own called cooperatives. Together, they could negotiate a better price for their grain or even build their own elevators and mills. In the 1860s a Minnesotan named Oliver Hudson Kelley started a farmers' group called the Order of the Patrons of Husbandry, popularly known as the Grange, which led a national movement for farmers' rights. Grange members fought for laws regulating how much the railroads could charge for shipping, shared new farming methods, and banded together to buy machinery at lower prices.

THE TWENTIETH CENTURY

In 1918 some workers and small farmers had started their own political party, called the Farmer-Labor Party, because they believed that neither the Democrats nor the Republicans did enough to help them. The Farmer-Labor Party reached full flower in the 1920s and 1930s, when two of Minnesota's governors, four U.S. senators from the state, and the majority of the state legislature were all party members.

Farming in Minnesota hit its low point during the Great Depression of the 1930s. Many farmers could not make any money at all. One farmer sent a 600-pound hog to Chicago by train, but the railroad charged more to ship it than he made from selling the animal. Prices for grain were so low that in 1932, some farmers went on strike. They blocked the roads, refusing to allow food into the cities.

Many farmers lost more than money—they lost their farms. Oftentimes, they had borrowed money to buy their land. When the price of corn fell from $0.80 to $0.10 a bushel, there was no way they could earn enough to repay the loans. The banks took back the farms and auctioned them off. Some farmers tried to prevent these sales by threatening judges and sheriffs. Others crowded the auctions and bought the farm, tools, and animals for mere pennies; anyone who tried to bid more was warned to keep silent. Having bought a farm at one of these "penny auctions," the farmers would simply give it back to the original owner.

Many other people also suffered during the Great Depression. Two-thirds of Minnesota's iron miners lost their jobs, and one-in-three factory workers in the Twin Cities was laid off. The Depression ended in the United States with the beginning of World War II. Minnesota's miners supplied iron for America's war effort, and farmers provided food for soldiers.

During the Great Depression young Minnesotans joined picket lines and demonstrations.

In 1944 the Democratic Party merged with the Farmer-Labor Party. Though not as radical as the old Farmer-Labor Party, the Democratic-Farmer-Labor Party (DFL) produced such popular liberal politicians as Hubert H. Humphrey, who was a leader in the national movement for civil rights. In 1964 Humphrey was elected vice president of the United States. Another DFL senator, Walter Mondale, was elected vice president in 1976.

The DFL's power has decreased since the 1970s, and Republicans have gained ground in the state. In 1998 Minnesota voters shocked the nation by electing the former professional wrestler Jesse "the Body" Ventura of the Reform Party as their governor, proving that the tradition of looking beyond the two major parties was alive and well in Minnesota. In that same election the Republicans took control from the DFL in the state's house of representatives.

THE NEW MILLENNIUM

Minnesotans bade farewell to the twentieth century and began the third millennium and twenty-first century during Jesse Ventura's administration (1999–2003). In spite of doom-and-gloom predictions for mismanagement, Minnesota survived and even thrived under the former wrestler. In 2001 he signed a law that funded the construction of Minnesota's first light-rail line. The first passengers rode the Hiawatha Line in 2004 from Nicollet Mall in Minneapolis to the Mall of America in Bloomington. Stops between these two points include many Minneapolis neighborhoods, Fort Snelling, and Minneapolis-St. Paul International Airport. City planners are proposing other light-rail lines that will connect the downtowns of Minneapolis and St. Paul and Minneapolis and St. Cloud.

In 2005 and 2006 Minneapolis experienced an arts and culture explosion. The Walker Art Center and the Children's Theatre Company (CTC) completed expansions of their already-famous buildings. During its expansion the Minneapolis Institute of Arts became physically connected to the CTC by an enclosed walkway. A new Guthrie Theater with three different types of stages opened at its new site on the Mississippi River. The original Guthrie had opened next to the Walker Art Center in 1963. On the University of Minnesota's Minneapolis campus the Weisman Art Museum announced

Bob Gibbons, Minnesota's Metro Transit director, said the Hiawatha Line raises "the visibility of all types of public transportation."

expansion plans designed by world-famous architect Frank O. Gehry. The Minneapolis Public Library welcomed patrons to its new five-story downtown facility. Except for the library, all the other projects were completely paid for by individuals and companies. Minneapolis taxpayers voted for an increase in their property taxes to build the downtown library.

Party politics remains an important part of Minnesota life. In October 2002 the Democratic U.S. senator Paul Wellstone, his wife, and their daughter were killed in a plane crash while campaigning for his reelection in November. Unfortunately, the memorial service for the Wellstones turned into a Democrat campaign rally. The former U.S. senator and former vice president Walter Mondale ran as the Democrat in Wellstone's place. St. Paul's Republican mayor Norm Coleman, however, won the U.S. Senate election by 49,000 votes.

In the same election Jesse Ventura chose not to run for reelection as governor. The Republican Tim Pawlenty beat out two other candidates to become Minnesota's thirty-ninth governor. Under him the state legislature passed a conceal-and-carry gun law that upset many people. In other developments Pawlenty increased Minnesota's foreign trade with Asian countries. In the 2006 general election Pawlenty was reelected for a second term as governor.

Also in that election, Keith Ellison, an African-American Muslim from Minneapolis, was elected to the U.S. House of Representatives. On January 4, 2007, he became the first Muslim to serve in Congress. After his official swearing-in with the 434 other representatives in the House chamber, he, like many other first-time representatives, had a second, unofficial swearing-in that was photographed with family and friends. Ellison took this unofficial oath of office with his hand on a copy of the Qur'an, the Muslim holy book.

Chapter Three

The Changing Faces of Minnesotans

According to the Minnesota writer Garrison Keillor, modesty is a characteristic of Minnesota's people, "a state of Germans and Scandinavians who believe in hard work, perseverance, and don't think you're somebody special, because you're not." Minnesotans have a reputation for being patient, humble, and extremely polite. The phrase "Minnesota Nice" is used to describe their famous courtesy.

In his book *How to Talk Minnesotan*, the humorist Howard Mohr jokes that a real Minnesotan will never accept food until the third offer. He includes the following as an example of such a conversation:

"Want a cup of coffee before you go?"
"No, I wouldn't want to put you out. I'll get by."
"You sure? Just made a fresh pot."
"You didn't have to go and do that."
"How about it, one cup?"
"Well, if it's going to hurt your feelings, but don't fill it full."

People from many cultures have made Minnesota their home.

This mild-mannered, low-key quality can be confusing to outsiders. One transplanted New Yorker, Barbara Graham, complained that when talking to a native Minnesotan, "Yah, then, I'm not feelin' too good" might well mean, "Help! I'm having a heart attack!" Others complain that being "nice" all the time means Minnesotans don't say what they're really feeling. Many people give as an example "the old Swedish farmer who loved his wife so much, he nearly told her."

Do all Minnesotans sound like the people in these jokes? As with many stereotypes, the answer is no, of course not. If they reveal anything, it is probably that Minnesotans love poking fun at themselves.

FROM FARAWAY LANDS

The stereotype of Minnesota as a land of Scandinavians and Germans is partly true: the state's three largest ethnic groups are Germans, Swedes, and Norwegians. Other groups, such as the descendants of Finnish, Italian, and eastern European immigrants who came to work on the Iron Range, also populate the state. Many Irish people settled in St. Paul, southeastern Minnesota, and the Red River valley. Some farm towns are filled with people of Czech and Polish heritage. In the late 1800s Russians and Ukrainians became farmers in southwestern Minnesota. Another wave of Russian immigrants arrived in the 1990s after the Soviet Union collapsed. Most of them were well educated and found professional positions in the Twin Cities.

Ashley Vlasek (left) practices dance steps at the Miss Czech Slovak USA Pageant.

SWEDISH MEATBALLS

This dish of meatballs in a creamy sauce was brought to Minnesota by Scandinavian immigrants. Today, it is popular throughout the state. Have an adult help you with this recipe.

1/2 cup milk

1 egg, slightly beaten

2 slices bread, crusts removed, torn into chunks

1 pound lean ground beef

1/2 pound ground pork

2 tablespoons onion, finely minced

1 teaspoon salt

1/2 teaspoon sugar

1/2 teaspoon black pepper

4 tablespoons butter

1 can condensed cream of chicken soup

1/2 can condensed tomato soup

1/2 soup can warm water

1. Combine the milk and egg. Add bread. Set aside to soak.

2. Combine the onions with the beef, pork, salt, sugar, and pepper in large a bowl. Mix slightly with hands. Add egg mixture and mix thoroughly.

3. Shape into small meatballs about the size of walnuts.

4. Heat butter in frying pan over medium heat. Brown meatballs, turning often to keep them round. Do not crowd pan.

5. Remove meatballs from pan. Add chicken soup, tomato soup, and water to pan, and stir thoroughly.

6. Place meatballs in a casserole dish. Pour sauce over top and bake for 20 minutes at 350 degrees.

ETHNIC MINNESOTA

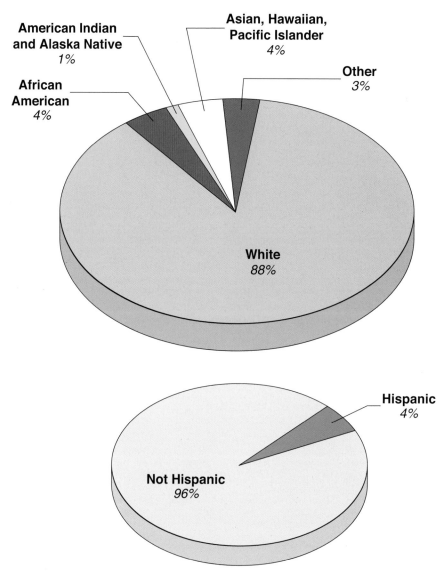

American Indian
and Alaska Native
1%

African
American
4%

Asian, Hawaiian,
Pacific Islander
4%

Other
3%

White
88%

Hispanic
4%

Not Hispanic
96%

Note: A person of Cuban, Mexican, Puerto Rican, South or Central American, or other Spanish culture or origin, regardless of race, is defined as Hispanic.

While European Americans still make up 88 percent of Minnesotans, this number has dropped from 94 percent in 1990 as more immigrants arrived from Africa and Asia. African Americans have lived in Minnesota since the 1700s. Many of them were fur traders. Currently, African Americans are Minnesota's largest minority group, making up 4 percent of the state's population. Since the 1980s, several thousand East Africans have settled in the Twin Cities, St. Cloud, and the southern Minnesota towns of Mankato, Owatonna, and Rochester. Most of them were refugees from civil wars and famine in Eritrea, Ethiopia, Somalia, and Sudan. Church and community groups reached out to help these refugees settle in their new country.

Longtime residents of Minnesota, African Americans make up 4 percent of the state's population.

People with Hispanic backgrounds make up 4 percent of Minnesota's population. Mexican farmworkers first arrived in great numbers during the 1920s. They mainly found jobs in sugar beet fields. Today, most of Minnesota's Hispanic population lives in the Twin Cities, while great numbers work in food-processing plants in the southern part of the state. Besides coming from Mexico, several thousand of Minnesota's Hispanics trace their ancestry to Cuba, Puerto Rico, and countries in South America.

These teens celebrate their Puerto Rican heritage at St. Paul's Cinco de Mayo festival.

Minnesota also has a large Asian community that makes up 3.5 percent of the state's population. Several thousand Indians, Chinese, and Koreans have settled in the Twin Cities and nearby suburbs, where many have careers in high-tech fields and health care. The largest Asian groups in Minnesota are the Vietnamese, Laotian, and Hmong peoples. In the late 1970s these people first found refuge in Minnesota after the United States ended its role in the Vietnam War. The Hmong lived in the highlands of Laos. These Southeast Asian people had helped the U.S. government during that war. When the United States pulled out of Vietnam, the Hmong were left to the mercy of their enemies, and thousands were killed. Church groups in Minnesota invited Hmong refugees to the Twin Cities. Church and community groups continue to help the Hmong, who were still moving to Minnesota in the early 2000s. Many Hmong have a hard time adjusting to life in their new home. Su Thao remembers stepping off a plane as a young boy in subzero weather wearing only sandals on his feet. In Laos he had hunted in the mountains and had ridden a water buffalo to school. In Minnesota he joined a Boy Scout troop and became the first Hmong Eagle Scout. The former Congressman Bruce Vento said, "I'm very proud of the fact that in St. Paul schools about 30 percent . . . are Southeast Asian. . . . They are going to be leaders in my state and they're going to be leaders in this country." Vento's prediction came true in 2002 when Mee Moua of St. Paul was elected to the Minnesota state senate. Her family fled Laos when she was five years old.

Customers buy produce at a farmer's market in Minneapolis that is run by Hmong farmers.

The influx of people from around the world has made Minneapolis much more cosmopolitan. In 1970 the city was 93 percent white. By 1990 the minority population had risen to 22 percent, and it continued to increase in the early 2000s. Adele Starr, a nurse practitioner in Minneapolis, said that her clinic has five full-time translators. "We have two Hmong/Laotian interpreters, one Somali interpreter, one Vietnamese interpreter, one Cambodian interpreter, and several people on our staff speak Spanish. It's like working in the United Nations. It's so interesting." By 2007, 72 percent of Minneapolis's public school children were nonwhite, and they spoke seventy-one different languages.

The newcomers have also spiced up the local cuisine. Twin Cities residents now have their pick of Mexican, Ethiopian, and Vietnamese restaurants. "Bland is boring. This is really cool," said Dale Hall of the squid, boiled quail eggs, and jelly grass he had just purchased from a Vietnamese food market.

MINNESOTA'S NATIVE AMERICANS

Minnesota's original inhabitants, the Santee Sioux and Ojibwe, make up only 1 percent of the state's population, about 59,000 people. At one time during the 1980s, Minneapolis had the largest Native-American population of any U.S. city. The American Indian Movement (AIM) began in Minneapolis. Today, about 40 percent of the state's Native Americans live in the Twin Cities. One-third of Minnesota's Native Americans live on reservations. The Ojibwe have seven large reservations in northern Minnesota; the Santee Sioux have four small ones in the southern part of the state. Some Ojibwe still collect wild rice on their reservation land. Many Ojibwe and Santee work in manufacturing plants that have been built on the reservations. Each reservation also has a resort complex with a gambling casino, bingo hall, hotel, and restaurants. Minnesota's Native Americans operate some of the country's most successful casinos. Income from casino gambling has built schools, museums, and health-care centers on some reservations. On other reservations casino earnings have been divided among tribal members, making some of them millionaires. "Now that we have casinos, more people are moving back to the reservation. . . . Which is good, because now we have a little bit more of an Indian community than we had before," said the Ojibwe Brenda Moose Boyd.

Over the years Minnesota's Native Americans have struggled with poverty and with adjusting to new traditions. At one time Native Americans were

Native Americans celebrate their culture at a local powwow in St. Paul.

forbidden to speak their native languages and were only taught in English. Today, only twenty-seven Santee Sioux in Minnesota can speak their native language. This might change if a Dakota version of Scrabble catches on. By playing this game, Santee Sioux children and adults can learn words in their native language. They can refer to a dictionary containing 2,500 Dakota words.

CELEBRATING TOGETHER

Minnesotans celebrate their many different traditions with hundreds of festivals. In addition to a Festival of Nations in St. Paul celebrating the city's ninety-five different ethnic groups, there are festivals for individual groups. Some of these festivals include Czech Kolacky Days in Montgomery, a German Oktoberfest in New Ulm, an Ojibwe powwow at the Mille Lacs Reservation, and Syttende Mai, a Norwegian independence day celebration in Wanamingo featuring a lutefisk dinner. Lutefisk, a Nordic dish made of cod soaked in lye, has achieved legendary status in Minnesota. Lutefisk is also known as "The piece of cod that surpasses all understanding."

For many a festival is simply a way to see old friends and celebrate small-town life. The North Morristown Picnic has been a Fourth of July tradition for more than one hundred years. "There aren't too many places like this anymore," said a woman from Kilkenny who came to dance to the polka music of the Six Fat Dutchmen. "I think that a lot of people like to go back to the more traditional celebrations their parents and grandparents had." Don Preuss of Waseca has been coming to the picnic for sixty years. "It's a real family-oriented deal," he said. "I think the church and school really help hold it together." Altogether, Minnesota celebrates about 1,600 festivals each year.

OUTDOOR FUN

Even in the heart of winter, Minnesotans aren't afraid to go outside and play. The journalist Dan Kaercher once wrote, "I'm still amazed at a simple fact of life in our region: the farther north you go, the more fun people have in winter." Pointing to a frozen lake, the Minnesotan Jane Gunsbury explained, "We have all this extra room in the winter. Might as well have fun with it!"

"PLEASE DO NOT DRILL HOLES IN THE ROADS"

Most people would be nervous about driving their car onto a frozen lake—and rightly so. But when the ice is 3 feet thick, as it can be in Minnesota, it's too inviting for some to pass up. Under all that ice, fish are swimming around. All you have to do is chop a hole, and you can go ice fishing.

Since it's too cold to sit outside all day, most ice fishermen drag buildings onto the ice and fish through holes in the floor. These shacks range from homemade plywood-and-tar paper shanties to heated, carpeted houses. The ice fisherman Jim Mackenthun can fish from his shanty while lying in bed and listening to the radio. While small lakes may sprout just a few old shacks, on Mille Lacs Lake (below), which is over 17 miles long, five thousand ice-fishing houses form a good-sized town. Neat roads are shoveled through the snow, and the buildings have driveways and street addresses. A road map warns ice fishermen, "Please do not drill holes in the roads."

Several lakes offer ice-fishing contests, where for a dollar, people willing to sit outdoors can try their luck. At Gull Lake nearly six thousand people pay $30 to trudge out on the ice in below-zero weather for the annual $150,000 Ice Fishing Extravaganza. They huddle over their fishing holes, trying to keep warm with propane heaters or by dancing to the music broadcast over loudspeakers. As Bob Michael said of his fellow ice fishermen, "This is behavior that's unique."

One thing many Minnesotans like to do is ride snowmobiles, which were invented in northern Minnesota. The state contains more than 18,000 miles of snowmobile trails. Betsy Hollister runs a coffeehouse in Nisswa along a 100-mile route from Brainerd to Bemidji, where snowmobilers stop and warm up by a fire. "Hot soup, hot coffee, and they're off. They can't wait to get back out there," she said.

Less noisy winter sports include snowshoeing and cross-country skiing. For something different, you can put on some skis, strap yourself to a sled dog, and go skijoring. "It's like waterskiing, but the

Minnesotans have many trails to choose from to enjoy snowshoeing.

boat is a dog, and the snow is the water," explained Shari Baker, who works at the Gunflint Lodge, which rents skijoring equipment.

Minnesota is the biggest hockey state in the country. In the winter Minnesotans can hose down a football field or shovel off a frozen lake, and they've got a hockey rink. Minnesota has more than two thousand amateur hockey clubs and has turned out more professional and Olympic hockey players than any other state. Most U.S. colleges need to import players from Canada for their teams, but the University of Minnesota once won a national championship with a team composed entirely of players born in Minnesota. The state's first professional hockey team was the North Stars. They played in Bloomington from 1967 to 1993. Surprisingly, this big hockey state was without a professional team until the Minnesota Wild started playing in 2000 in St. Paul.

In summer Minnesotans make full use of their lakes. About 750,000 boats are registered in Minnesota—one for every six people—and one of every four Minnesotans has a fishing license. According to one poll, six of ten adult Minnesotans made an overnight trip to a lake within the past year. For many residents, "a dock, a lake, a cabin, and a fishing boat is kind of like standard equipment," said the Minnesota native Chris Stellar. On summer weekends the highways are full of families going "up north to the lake."

Youth hockey leagues are serious business in Minnesota.

POPULATION DENSITY

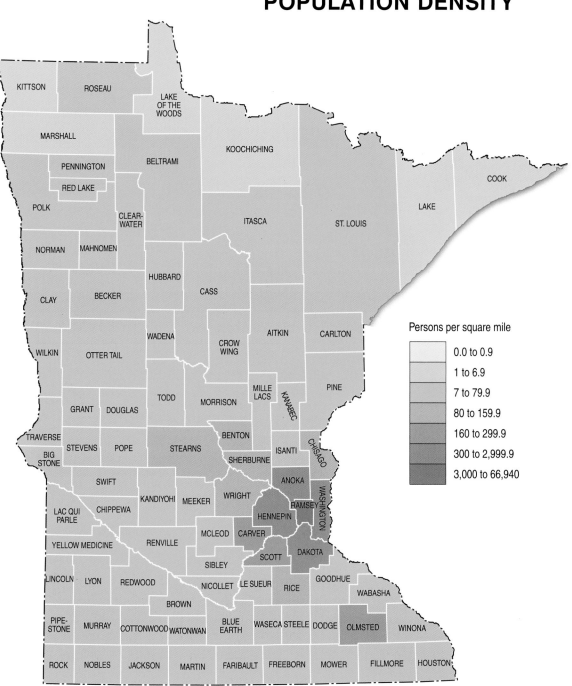

Persons per square mile

	0.0 to 0.9
	1 to 6.9
	7 to 79.9
	80 to 159.9
	160 to 299.9
	300 to 2,999.9
	3,000 to 66,940

KITTSON
ROSEAU
LAKE OF THE WOODS
MARSHALL
KOOCHICHING
PENNINGTON
BELTRAMI
RED LAKE
COOK
POLK
CLEARWATER
ITASCA
LAKE
NORMAN
MAHNOMEN
ST. LOUIS
HUBBARD
CLAY
BECKER
CASS
WADENA
AITKIN
CARLTON
WILKIN
OTTER TAIL
CROW WING
MILLE LACS
PINE
TRAVERSE
GRANT
DOUGLAS
TODD
MORRISON
KANABEC
BENTON
STEVENS
POPE
STEARNS
ISANTI
CHISAGO
BIG STONE
SHERBURNE
SWIFT
ANOKA
KANDIYOHI
MEEKER
WRIGHT
RAMSEY
WASHINGTON
LAC QUI PARLE
CHIPPEWA
HENNEPIN
YELLOW MEDICINE
RENVILLE
MCLEOD
CARVER
SCOTT
DAKOTA
SIBLEY
LINCOLN
LYON
REDWOOD
NICOLLET
LE SUEUR
RICE
GOODHUE
WABASHA
BROWN
PIPESTONE
MURRAY
COTTONWOOD
WATONWAN
BLUE EARTH
WASECA
STEELE
DODGE
OLMSTED
WINONA
ROCK
NOBLES
JACKSON
MARTIN
FARIBAULT
FREEBORN
MOWER
FILLMORE
HOUSTON

CITIES, SUBURBS, AND EXURBS

From the 1950s to the late 1990s Minneapolis and St. Paul lost thousands of residents to the suburbs. From the late 1990s to the present, however, the Twin Cities have regained population, mainly from the great number of African and Asian immigrants who settled there. In fact, in 2005 Minnesota received more immigrants than any other state, with most of them settling in Minneapolis or St. Paul. After completing college, many children of farmers from rural Minnesota and neighboring states also moved to Minnesota cities, where they found jobs.

The suburbs that boomed in the 1950s through 1970s, such as Bloomington, Brooklyn Park, and Burnsville, have become cities in their own right. In recent years they have also benefited from increased immigrant populations. In addition, some of the state's towns, such as Mankato and St. Cloud, are now considered to be cities. In contrast, other towns, such as Stillwater and Hastings, are called exurbs. They were once considered small towns. Now they are far-out suburbs, or exurbs, of the Twin Cities. These exurbs are linked to the major cities by a string of suburban development and good highways. Former Minnesotans who return for visits home are amazed at the growth and development that's taken place in the past twenty years.

Chapter Four

A Progressive Government

Besides its "nice" people, Minnesota is also known for clean, progressive government. Because Minnesotans believe in such traditional values as civic responsibility and lending a hand to a neighbor, they elect leaders and representatives with the same values.

These leaders and representatives usually follow the wishes of the voters. If they don't, Minnesotans turn them out of office or start another political party. Though politicians from other states may look at Minnesotans as old-fashioned, Minnesota voters and politicians are not afraid to try new ideas. Minnesota has led the way on many reforms in education, environmental protection, and law enforcement.

INSIDE GOVERNMENT

Minnesota is governed by its original constitution, which was drawn up before Minnesota became a state in 1858. Although many states have

Minnesota's legislature works on new bills, taxes, and budgets at the State Capitol in St. Paul.

totally rewritten their constitutions, Minnesotans have changed theirs by adding more than one hundred amendments. The state legislature recommends the amendments, but the voters must approve them in a general election. According to the constitution, Minnesota's government has three branches: executive, legislative, and judicial.

Executive Branch

The head of the executive branch is the governor, who is elected to a four-year term. Unlike many states, Minnesota does not set term limits for the governor. The governor and his choice for lieutenant governor run as a team. The lieutenant governor would serve as governor if anything happened to the governor. Minnesota has not had a woman governor

Governor Tim Pawlenty and Lieutenant Governor Carol Molnau celebrate victory on election night, 2006.

yet, although the past few governors have selected women to run as lieutenant governor. Other elected officials in the executive branch are the secretary of state, attorney general, and state auditor. The elected office of state treasurer was eliminated in 2003, according to a 1998 amendment to the constitution.

Minnesota's governor has many powers. He appoints the heads of twenty-five commissions and state departments. He signs laws passed by the legislature or blocks them with vetoes. The legislature can override the governor's veto if two-thirds of its members agree. The governor can call special sessions of the legislature and can call out the state National Guard in emergencies.

Legislative Branch

The legislative branch of Minnesota's government consists of a two-chamber legislature. The upper chamber is the senate, with 67 members who serve four-year terms; and the lower chamber is the house of representatives, with 134 members who serve two-year terms. From 1913 to 1972 senators and representatives could not run as part of a political party. Instead, Democrats and Farmer Laborites ran as "Liberals," and Republicans ran as "Conservatives." Since 1972 they have again been running with party labels. From 1972 to 2006 the Democratic-Farmer-Labor Party (DFL) has controlled the state senate. From 1999 to 2006 the Republicans held a strong majority in the state house of representatives. Control of the house of representatives swings back and forth between Republicans and Democrats.

The legislature passes bills that must be signed into law by the governor. If the governor vetoes a bill, a two-thirds majority in each chamber of the legislature can override the governor's veto. The legislature also sets taxes and controls the state budget.

In recent years the legislature has passed several laws that protect children and teenagers. In 2005 a law was passed that required children under ten years of age to wear a life jacket when boating on state waters. Another 2005 law required that a person be at least twelve years old to operate a motorized foot scooter and that the operator wear a helmet. In 2006 the legislature passed a law that prohibited drivers under the age of eighteen years from using a cell phone—even a hands-free version—while driving.

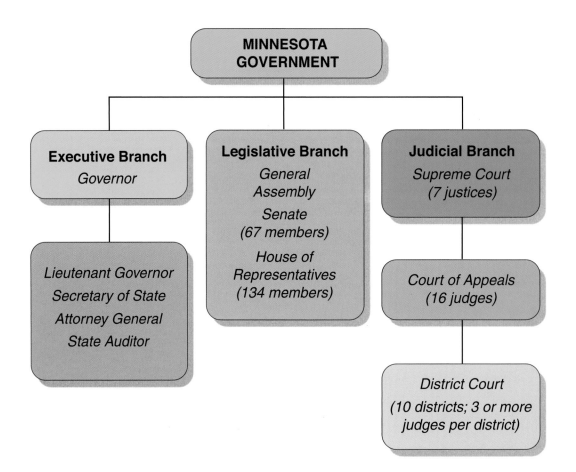

Judicial Branch

The state's highest court is the supreme court, composed of seven justices elected to six-year terms. Beneath it is the court of appeals, with sixteen judges who are also elected for six-year terms. Minnesota's district court is divided into ten districts. Each district has at least three judges, who are elected to six-year terms. County courts, municipal courts, and justices of the peace are other divisions of Minnesota's judicial branch. The decisions of lower courts can be appealed to higher courts for review, all the way up to the state supreme court.

Minnesota's best-known judge is Alan Page, one of the greatest football players in history. As a member of the powerful Minnesota Vikings team (1967–1981) that played in four Super Bowls, Page became the first defensive player ever named the league's Most Valuable Player. Page attended the University of Minnesota's Law School between football seasons and received his law degree in 1978. When he retired from the sport, he became a lawyer and then a judge. He has been a Minnesota supreme court justice since 1993. Page has spoken to thousands of schoolchildren, reminding them that their education is a lot more important than sports. Currently, the state's supreme court has two women serving as justices.

Alan Page, a former professional football player for the Minnesota Vikings, became a Minnesota supreme court justice in 1993.

SUPPORTING SCHOOLS, HEALTH CARE, AND ONE ANOTHER

Minnesotans are proud of their commitment to keeping Minnesota a nice place to live for everyone. "We are not like a lot of other states. We want to be thought of as a very progressive state, but we don't want to be thought of as a big state. We're willing to pay more taxes for certain things, and we're very prideful of those things," the said prominent businessman Glen Taylor.

Minnesotans pay some of the highest taxes in the nation. One thing Minnesotans get for their high taxes is an excellent school system. Minnesota ranks near the top of all the states in the percentage of students who graduate from high school and among the top five states in college admission test scores. More than 92 percent of adult Minnesotans are high school graduates. This is the largest percentage in the fifty states. About 32 percent of adult Minnesotans hold a bachelor's degree—also above the national average. Conversely, only 3.8 percent of Minnesota's students drop out of school. This is below the national average. Almost half the state budget goes toward education.

Education Minnesota, an organization of 70,000 educators, has a mission to "become the pre-eminent source of excellence in teaching and learning in Minnesota."

Another reason for the success of Minnesota schools is a willingness to experiment. For example, the first charter schools in the country opened in Minnesota in 1991. Charter schools are run with tax money but are operated by teachers and parents rather than by a school board. Minnesota students are not limited to attending schools in their own district, because the state offers open enrollment across school districts. As the Minneapolis schools superintendent proudly explained, "We have more choices. In this district you can go to an open school, a Montessori school, a continuous-progress school, a regular school, a math-science-technology school, a language-immersion school, a liberal-arts magnet, an aerospace magnet, a fine-arts magnet." In hard-to-reach rural areas of Minnesota, students have been taking classes via television for years and now take them over the Internet.

Building schools and training teachers has been important in Minnesota since its territorial and early statehood years. For example, the University of Minnesota in Minneapolis was founded in 1851 as a school to prepare students for admission to college. In 1868 it became a four-year college. Now the U of M also has campuses in St. Paul, Duluth, Morris, Rochester, and Crookston. In addition, Minnesota has forty-five other tax-supported universities, colleges, and technical schools as well as sixty-one private institutions of higher learning.

Minnesota's interest in health care also has a long history. One of the world's most famous medical centers is the Mayo Clinic, in Rochester, Minnesota. It began as a small surgical clinic in 1883 under Dr. William Mayo and his sons, Drs. Charles and William Mayo. Today, the Mayo Clinic has grown to include several hospitals and more than two thousand doctors who care for 400,000 people from around the world each year. The University of Minnesota Medical Center in Minneapolis is known for its advances in heart care. The state has many other fine hospitals in its cities and large towns.

In 2002 the state began a program to entice doctors and pharmacists to work in small towns. By serving patients in rural areas, these doctors have their student loans reduced by thousands of dollars each year. Besides having great hospitals and doctors, more Minnesotans are covered by health insurance than are people in the nation as a whole. Perhaps because of their excellent health care and insurance coverage, Minnesota's death rates from cancer and heart disease are lower than the national averages.

Minnesotans' commitment to taking care of one another and their communities has not made them immune to problems. But they try to respond in creative ways that consider the needs of all. For instance, in 1996 new federal laws forced people

Rochester's Mayo Clinic is a not-for-profit facility dedicated to the treatment of most illnesses.

off welfare in the hope that they would start working to support themselves. Although Minnesota pushed people to find work, it also supplied money to solve the problems that prevented them from working. "If it's child care, let's connect you with the basic sliding-fee child care so you can avoid going on welfare. If it's because your car broke down, then let's fix the car," said Deborah Huskings of the Minnesota Department of Human Services.

MINNESOTA BY COUNTY

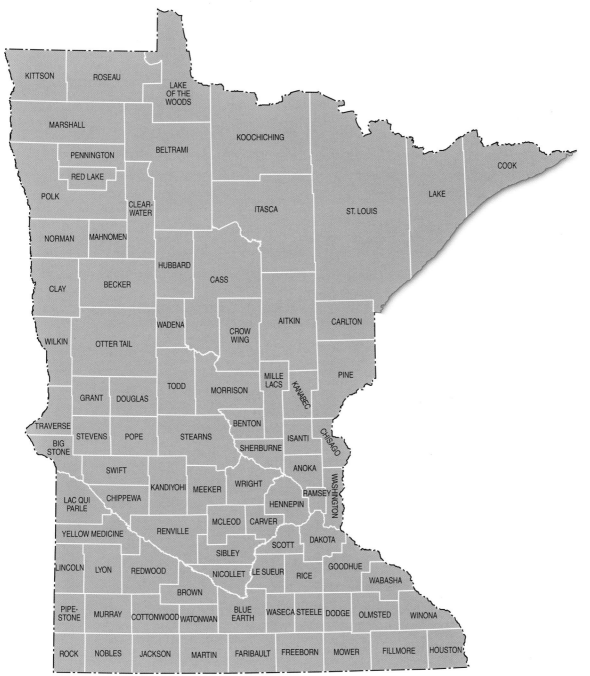

FIGHTING CRIME

In the mid-1990s Minnesotans—used to seeing themselves as peaceful and law-abiding—were stunned when the murder rate in Minneapolis soared. Criminal gangs were moving into the city, and a third of the inmates in Minneapolis's Hennepin County Jail had lived in Minnesota for less than five years. Minneapolis responded to this influx of criminals by targeting gangs and people who committed crimes while out on parole for other convictions. Previously, those who violated parole faced few consequences. Now, repeat offenders quickly found themselves back in jail. Over the next few years the murder rate dropped sharply.

But true to its liberal traditions, Minneapolis did not stop at simply "getting tough" on crime. The city also worked hard to prevent kids from turning to crime in the first place. School programs, recreation programs, and neighborhood block clubs were all enlisted to provide healthy places for kids to spend time. While other states responded to crime by simply building more prisons, Minnesota's corrections commissioner, Fred LaFleur, insisted that Minnesota "can't build our way out of the situation—that's folly." He argued that it is cheaper and more effective to help troubled families by offering parenting classes and skills training to help keep people from turning to crime in the first place.

Crime prevention in Minnesota begins with educational programs for children.

CAMERAS CATCH CRIMINALS

Most of Minnesota's small towns cannot afford a full-time police force, which might cost $100,000 or more each year. Instead, some towns rely on officers from the county sheriff's office, which can be several miles away. Other towns might have an arrangement to get help from law enforcement in another town a few miles away. The town of Sanborn, with a population of just over four hundred, in southwestern Redwood County decided to try something different.

In November 2005 Mayor Charlie Hosack, who was a retired police officer, convinced the town to install nine security cameras on Sanborn's streets. Most of the $29,000 cost of the cameras and hookups was paid for through donations. The cameras are aimed at the streets, and the video feeds to a television set in the office of Sanborn's city clerk in City Hall and to a set in the Redwood County sheriff's office. The televisions' screens are divided into nine squares—one for each camera. The cameras catch everything from teenagers hot-rodding through town late at night to drug deals.

Since the cameras were installed, the number of complaints about crimes has dropped to about zero. When a crime does occur, the city clerk and mayor rerun the tapes from a particular time and day and then call the sheriff, who investigates. No one sits and watches the television screens twenty-four hours a day, seven days a week. About the camera system Mayor Sanborn commented, "It's a pair of eyes, if you need 'em. But we've only had to check it a couple of times."

Chapter Five

From Traditional to High Tech

During the past twenty years many northern and midwestern states have experienced economic problems because they depended too much on one main crop or one major industry. In contrast, Minnesota already had developed a diverse economy that included a wide variety of agricultural and manufacturing products as well as many kinds of service businesses. While the business owners in many other states were slow to shift from manufacturing to service-based businesses, Minnesota's business community had already started that process in the 1950s. During that process, however, Minnesotans did not turn their backs on farming and mining. Instead, those traditional industries were maintained as important parts of the state's total economy.

Because of its diverse economy, Minnesota has a low unemployment rate—much lower than that of the United States as a whole. In many industries Minnesotans' wages are higher than the national average.

Farming is an important industry in rural Minnesota.

In 2004 Minnesota's earnings from goods and services produced in the state ranked seventeenth among the fifty states. These earnings continue to increase each year at a rate above the national average. Because of these figures, it's not surprising that Minnesota is home to eighteen Fortune 500 companies. Some of the best-known retail, insurance, manufacturing, banking, and transportation businesses can be found in Minnesota, such as Target, Best Buy, St. Paul Travelers, 3M, Supervalu, U.S. Bancorp, Northwest Airlines, and General Mills.

MINNESOTA WORKFORCE

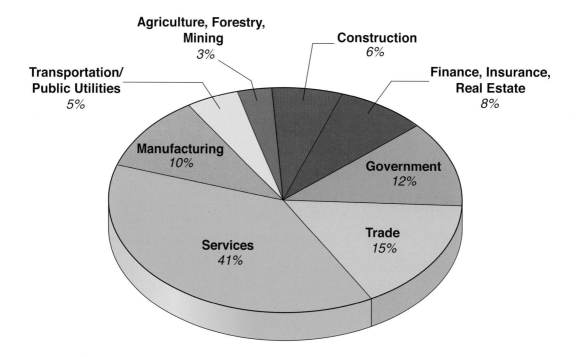

Agriculture, Forestry, Mining
3%

Construction
6%

Transportation/
Public Utilities
5%

Finance, Insurance,
Real Estate
8%

Manufacturing
10%

Government
12%

Services
41%

Trade
15%

FARMING, MINING, AND FORESTRY

Many Minnesotans still work in the state's traditional industries of farming, mining, and forestry. Farmland covers more than half the state, with most of it lying in western and southern Minnesota. This is some of the country's richest farmland, which helps give Minnesota one of the highest incomes from farm products in the fifty states. Minnesota's top moneymaking crops are soybeans and corn. But Minnesota's farmers grow more green peas, oats, and sugar beets than any other state. Other important crops are barley, flaxseed, potatoes, sunflowers, sweet corn, wheat, and wild rice. Apples are the leading fruit crop. Only Wisconsin outproduces Minnesota in dairy products, which include milk, butter, cheese, and ice cream. Hogs and cattle are the state's most valuable livestock, but Minnesota raises more turkeys than any other state. Other livestock products include chickens, eggs, sheep, and lambs. About 100,000 Minnesotans earn their living working on farms.

One of Minnesota's top crops is corn.

FARM STATE FUN

If you're lucky enough to be in the Twin Cities in late August, you can join the 1.5 million people who visit the Minnesota State Fair each year. The fair has all the traditional attractions, including cotton candy, carnival rides, and prize-winning pickles and pies, plus unique Minnesota treats such as "walleye pike on a stick," an original way to enjoy one of Minnesota's most popular fish. You can also try a popular snack in dairy country: deep-fried cheese curds. Leo Berg, the president of the Minnesota Festivals and Events Association, said that at a fair, "people like to eat something they are not going to eat every day of the year."

There are 15,000 animals at the fair, from llamas to horses, pigs, sheep, and chickens of every imaginable color—and, of course, cows. In the Moo Booth a dairy farmer tells visitors that "a 1,400-pound cow will eat enough to produce 115 pounds of manure every day." Other cow-related attractions include a life-size human head carved from an 85-pound hunk of butter and a tanker truck that sells all the fresh milk (plain or chocolate) you can drink for $1.00.

Iron ore is Minnesota's leading mining product, and Minnesota leads the other states in producing this mineral. The ore is now found in taconite rock taken from the mighty Mesabi open-pit mine. From there the taconite is shipped to the Northshore Mining plant in Silver Bay on Lake Superior, where the iron is extracted and formed into pellets. Iron is mainly used in the production of steel. Because U.S. companies have been importing cheaper Asian and European steel, many U.S. steel plants have closed, reducing the need for Minnesota's iron ore. To combat this problem, Minnesota's iron-ore industry has started exporting iron pellets to other countries, such as China.

A power shovel loads a truck with raw taconite ore.

Granite is Minnesota's second most valuable mineral and is quarried mainly near St. Cloud and in the western Minnesota River valley. Limestone and sandstone are quarried in southern Minnesota. Altogether, about seven thousand Minnesotans are employed in the mining and quarrying industries.

Forestry makes up a small part of Minnesota's economy today. Only one-third of the state remains forested, with much of it in state and national forestlands. About nine hundred loggers cut down trees and transport the logs by truck to paper and lumber mills. The main trees used by those industries are aspens and pines. The logging companies now have programs to replant the harvested areas so that new trees will grow.

2005 GROSS STATE PRODUCT: $235 Million

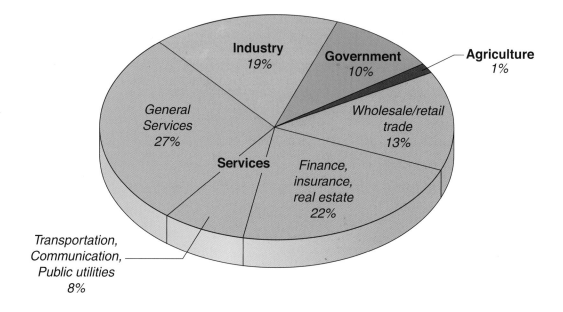

Industry 19%

Government 10%

Agriculture 1%

General Services 27%

Wholesale/retail trade 13%

Services

Finance, insurance, real estate 22%

Transportation, Communication, Public utilities 8%

MANUFACTURING

By 1948 manufacturing had become the state's leading industry, nudging agriculture into second place. Food processing has always been a leading manufacturing business in Minnesota. Mills, dairies, canneries, and refineries turned Minnesota's agricultural products into flour, cereals, cake mixes, butter, cheeses, canned vegetables, oils, and granulated sugar. Although the St. Anthony Falls are no longer surrounded by flour mills, the world's largest milling company, General Mills, still maintains its headquarters in Minneapolis. The shelves of almost every supermarket in the country hold General Mills products: Gold Medal flour, Betty Crocker baking mixes, and many kinds of cereals, including Wheaties and Cheerios. Two other well-known Minnesota food brands, Pillsbury and Green Giant, are now owned by General Mills. Other Minnesota food processors are Land O'Lakes in Arden Hills, best known for its butter; Hormel in Austin, which is famous for Spam, ham, and bacon products; and Schwan Food in Marshall, which makes and delivers its premium ice creams directly to homes.

Besides foods, Minnesota's factories produce machinery and transportation equipment. For example, Toro Industries in Bloomington makes power mowers, leaf blowers, and snow throwers. Alliant Techsystems in Edina produces rocket motors. Snowmobiles and all-terrain vehicles are made by rivals Polaris in Roseau and Arctic Cat in Thief River Falls. Several companies also build fishing boats, pontoon boats, and speedboats, which are used on Minnesota's many lakes.

Twin Cities companies are leaders in high-tech industries, which are Minnesota's biggest manufacturing moneymakers. The move to high tech started in the 1970s with computer makers Control Data and Cray Research. Now, several software companies line the expressways in the Twin Cities' suburbs. Another area of high-tech manufacturing is medical

Technicians wire a Cray supercomputer.

instruments and supplies. Engineers and scientists at Medtronic invented the heart pacemaker. Other high-tech fields include the manufacture of electronic equipment, computers and office equipment, and scientific instruments. In 2000 Minnesota ranked seventh among the states for its high-tech payroll. It also ranked fourth in the number of U.S. patents issued. Minnesota is able to take the lead in these highly competitive industries because it has a highly educated workforce.

Perhaps one of Minnesota's best-known manufacturers is 3M, with such famous products as Scotch Tape and Post-it Notes. Other Minnesota-made products used throughout the country include Deluxe checks from Shoreview, Andersen windows from Bayport, and Marvin windows from Warroad. Paper and wood products are also important manufactured products.

EARNING A LIVING

Natural Resources

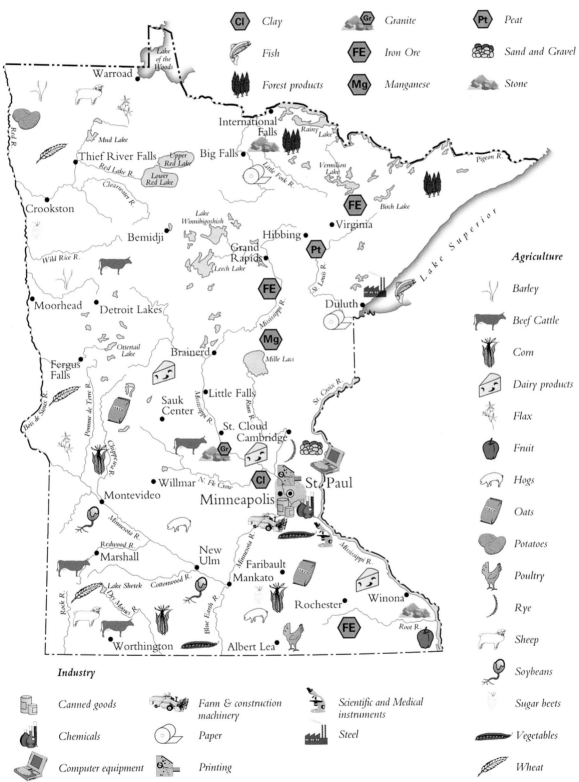

Cl Clay	**Gr** Granite	**Pt** Peat
Fish	**FE** Iron Ore	Sand and Gravel
Forest products	**Mg** Manganese	Stone

Lake of the Woods

Warroad

Red R.

International Falls

Rainy Lake

Mud Lake

Thief River Falls

Big Falls

Little Fork R.

Vermilion Lake

Pigeon R.

Upper Red Lake

Red Lake R.

Lower Red Lake

Clearwater R.

Crookston

Lake Winnibigoshish

Bemidji

Wild Rice R.

Grand Rapids

FE

Virginia

Pt

Hibbing

Birch Lake

Lake Superior

Leech Lake

St. Louis R.

Moorhead

Detroit Lakes

FE

Duluth

Mississippi R.

Ottertail Lake

Brainerd

Mg

Mille Lacs

Fergus Falls

Bois de Sioux R.

Pomme de Terre R.

Sauk Center

Little Falls

Mississippi R.

Rum R.

St. Croix R.

Chippewa R.

St. Cloud

Cambridge

Gr

Willmar

N. Fk. Crow

Cl

St. Paul

Montevideo

Minneapolis

Minnesota R.

Redwood R.

Marshall

New Ulm

Faribault

Minnesota R.

Mississippi R.

Rock R.

Lake Shetek

Cottonwood R.

Mankato

Rochester

Winona

Des Moines R.

Blue Earth R.

Root R.

FE

Worthington

Albert Lea

Agriculture

	Barley
	Beef Cattle
	Corn
	Dairy products
	Flax
	Fruit
	Hogs
	Oats
	Potatoes
	Poultry
	Rye
	Sheep
	Soybeans
	Sugar beets
	Vegetables
	Wheat

Industry

Canned goods	Farm & construction machinery	Scientific and Medical instruments
Chemicals	Paper	Steel
Computer equipment	Printing	

SERVICE INDUSTRIES

Service industries make up the largest part of Minnesota's economy. Trade—retail, wholesale, and international—is an important service industry. Three of the country's largest retail companies—Target Corporation, Best Buy, and Supervalu Stores—are headquartered in the Twin Cities area. Retail stores sell directly to the public. Supervalu also owns other national grocery chains, such as Albertsons and Jewel. In recent years international trade, especially with Asian countries, has grown quickly for Minnesota. Computers, electronic equipment, machinery, and transportation equipment were the top goods exported from Minnesota. Canada, China, Ireland, and Japan are the leading buyers of Minnesota goods.

Finance, transportation, restaurants, and hotels are other parts of Minnesota's service industry. With the Ninth Federal Reserve District in Minneapolis, the Twin Cities area is an important financial center. U.S. Bancorp is a major national bank based in Minneapolis. Large insurance companies include St. Paul Travelers, Thrivent, and Federated Mutual Insurance. Trains, planes, and buses are important means of transportation that keep Minnesotans and freight moving. Railroads include the former Great Northern line, now called the Burlington Northern Santa Fe, that connects the Twin Cities with Chicago to the east and Seattle to the west. The Greyhound Bus Line got its start in Hibbing in 1914. Northwest Airlines, one of the country's five largest airlines, began in Minneapolis in 1926 and now is headquartered in Eagan. People in the Midwest who like barbecued food have made Minneapolis-based Famous Dave's—well, famous! Buca di Beppo, another national restaurant chain based in Minneapolis, specializes in Italian food. Carlson Companies of Minnetonka, leaders in the travel, restaurant, and hotel businesses, own the chain of Radisson luxury hotels.

Northwest Airlines, based in Eagan, serves more than 900 cities and 160 countries.

Tourists enjoy the sights and sounds of Minnesota, contributing more than $9 billion to the state's economy each year.

In the 2000s more than thirteen million out-of-state tourists visited Minnesota each year. About the same number of Minnesotans vacationed or took trips within the state. Altogether, tourists spend more than $9 billion each year in the state. The top-five favorite tourist activities are shopping at the Mall of America, taking scenic tours, sightseeing in the Twin Cities, fishing, and visiting parks. About 130,000 people work in tourism-related jobs at hotels, resorts, state parks, and restaurants. Tourism is a key source of jobs in the north, where Voyageurs National Park and the Boundary Waters Canoe Area Wilderness preserve hundreds of unspoiled lakes. People come from all over the country to canoe in the Boundary Waters. For now the Boundary Waters remains one of the few places in the United States where people can canoe all day and hear only the splash of their paddles, the rustle of the wind in the trees, and perhaps the laughing call of a loon.

Chapter Six

A Tour of Minnesota

If a tour of Minnesota started with an airplane ride to the Twin Cities, the first view of the state might be a wide, flat stretch of farmland that looks like a patchwork quilt. Out of the fields would finally appear an expanse of houses with several lakes nestled among them and a winding river leading to a cluster of tall, glimmering buildings.

THE TWIN CITIES

Upon landing at Minneapolis-St. Paul International Airport, the tour would start at nearby Fort Snelling. The old stone fort has been restored to look the way it did in 1827. Visitors can watch a blacksmith at work and talk to guides dressed as a surgeon or a trader's wife. Soldiers in 1820s uniforms fire muskets, and the gift shop sells the kind of candy people ate in frontier days. Nearby, sheltered by the steep, rocky banks of the Minnesota River, is a peaceful park where hikers and cross-country skiers share miles of trails with white-tailed deer and other wildlife.

Next, historic Minnehaha Falls in Minneapolis is a must-see on any tour of the Twin Cities. *Minnehaha* means "laughing water" (it's easy to remember because of the *haha*). Over the falls the water meanders down

Begin a tour of Minnesota at Itasca State Park, where the great Mississippi River begins.

No tour of Minneapolis would be complete without a visit to the 53-foot Minnehaha Falls.

Minnehaha Creek into the Mississippi River. The nearby John H. Stevens House Museum, built in 1850, may have been the first house in Minneapolis. In it Minneapolis was named, its government and school districts were organized, its streets were mapped, and important meetings with the Santee Sioux were held. One day in 1896 Minneapolis schools closed so that more than seven thousand schoolchildren could help move the house from its original location in downtown Minneapolis to Minnehaha Park. The children took turns pulling the house on its 6-mile journey.

The Minneapolis Institute of Arts, featuring artwork from around the world, is linked to the dazzling Children's Theatre. Minneapolis's Walker Art Center specializes in modern art. Its collection features, for example, a 20-foot bag of French fries. Outside, visitors can stroll through a garden filled with more than forty sculptures, including one of a gigantic cherry perched on the end of a spoon. Even more modern

Spoonbridge and Cherry *was designed by Claes Oldenburg and Coosje van Bruggen. Oldenburg said, "Very often I am sitting at dinner . . . I get very inspired when I eat."*

is the whimsical Frank Gehry–designed Frederick R. Weisman Art Museum at the University of Minnesota. This building looks like a shiny aluminum toy. University of Minnesota students call it "the Tin Can."

St. Paul's Como Park contains a small zoo and a sparkling glass conservatory filled year-round with lush plants and flowers. Also in St. Paul is the terrific Children's Museum, where kids can climb through a maze of tunnels, deliver a television newscast, and operate the controls of a large crane. Nearby are two other great museums: the Minnesota History Center and the Science Museum of Minnesota. Of course, most visitors to St. Paul also take time for a tour of the State Capitol.

The Mall of America in the suburb of Bloomington, Minnesota's fifth-largest city, draws more visitors than anywhere else in the state. Why would forty million people a year want to see a mall? For starters, with more than five hundred stores, it's the biggest mall in the entire country. It's big enough for trees to grow inside it. Nestled among the trees is a 7-acre amusement park with seventeen rides, including a roller coaster that zooms above the trees' branches. On Saturday nights so many people fill the mall that it would rank as the third-biggest city in the state.

Wherever visitors go in the Twin Cities, they aren't far from a river or lake. In summer they can go swimming or canoeing, or watch a band playing in a lakeside park—the music wafting out across the water. In winter they can go ice-skating on a frozen lake, then head downtown to warm up. Stores in the Twin Cities are connected by glass "skyways" that allow people to walk from building to building without ever going outside. This can make a big difference when the temperature is below zero. The downtowns of Minneapolis and St. Paul each have 5 miles of these elevated public walkways—more than any other city in the world.

Besides hundreds of shops, the Mall of America includes a theme park (above), an aquarium, and a speedway.

Depending on the time of year, visitors and Minnesotans can take in several professional sporting events. The Wild play hockey at the Xcel Energy Center in St. Paul. The Lynx, the women's pro-basketball team, and the Timberwolves, the men's NBA team, shoot hoops at the Target Center in Minneapolis. The Vikings score touchdowns, and the Twins hit home runs at the Hubert H. Humphrey Metrodome in Minneapolis. Earl McDowell remarked that "for the past decade, Minnesota politicians have been arguing about building a new Twins' stadium." Finally, in 2006 the members of both the house and the senate agreed to build a new stadium in downtown Minneapolis—to open in 2010. The Vikings also are lobbying for a new football stadium.

Many Minnesotans enjoy watching the Vikings during football season.

SOUTH OF THE TWIN CITIES

After enjoying culture, shopping, and sports in the Twin Cities, the tour proceeds south to Northfield. In this town the notorious gang of bank robbers led by Jesse James finally met their match. The Northfield bank the gang tried to rob is now a museum, with guides that explain exactly how everything happened.

JESSE JAMES INVADES NORTHFIELD

In 1876 Jesse James and his gang headed north from their base in Missouri to rob the First National Bank in quiet Northfield. The Minnesota townsfolk turned out to be a lot tougher than the gang expected. To their amazement, Joseph Lee Heywood, a substitute cashier, refused to unlock the vault—even with a gun to his head. The gang killed him without getting any money. Another bank employee was shot in the shoulder as he ran away, but by that time the alarm was out. Local businessmen grabbed their guns and fired on the robbers. Two members of the gang were shot dead in the street. The rest fled. Dozens of angry farmers and businessmen joined posses that hunted down the fleeing robbers. Only Frank and Jesse James escaped; Cole, Jim, and Bob Younger were all caught, ending the James-Younger gang forever. The citizens of Northfield are so proud of putting an end to the murderous James-Younger gang that they reenact the event each year in the Defeat of Jesse James Days festival, which draws 100,000 people.

Just south of Northfield is Nerstrand-Big Woods State Park. Protected since 1945, this forest is one of the last remaining patches of the Big Woods that once covered several states. Laura Ingalls Wilder described life among the towering hardwoods in *Little House in the Big Woods*, her first book about her pioneer childhood. From the Wisconsin forest Laura moved to Minnesota, which she described in *On the Banks of Plum Creek*. Fans of the Little House books can visit her former home in Walnut Grove, Minnesota. For a taste of pioneer life visitors can spend a night nearby in an actual sod house, made of chunks of earth.

The rushing streams and rocky river bluffs of Minnesota's southeast corner make it a particularly scenic region. The beautiful river town of Wabasha contains the state's oldest hotel that's still in use. The Anderson House Hotel has been accepting guests since 1856; today, the hotel lets you choose a cat to take to your room with you.

North of Wabasha the Mississippi widens to form Lake Pepin, an expanse of water nearly 30 miles long and 3 miles wide. It's a great place for fishing, sailing, motorboating, and waterskiing. In fact, waterskiing was invented there in 1922, when the eighteen-year-old Ralph Samuelson strapped some wooden snow skis on his feet to see what would happen when he was dragged behind a boat. Apparently he enjoyed himself because people have been doing it ever since. Farther south a fascinating site is Niagara Cave, which contains a 60-foot-high underground waterfall.

ON THE PRAIRIE

Farther west the hills end, and the earth becomes flat. It's mostly farms now, but it's not hard to imagine what the prairie was like when the Santee Sioux roamed the land, hunting buffalo. At the Jeffers Petroglyphs, rocks poking up out of the prairie bear almost two thousand pictures, some as much as five thousand years old, carved by Native Americans. Various carvings depict bison, turtles, wolves, bows and arrows, and people.

THE LEGEND OF PIPESTONE

The practice of smoking tobacco originated with the North American Indians. For them smoking was a sacred act that connected them to the spirit world. This story tells how the Great Spirit brought the Indians the first pipe.

Long ago, the Great Spirit gathered all the different tribes beneath a red ridge of rock. Standing on the edge, he broke a piece from the wall and kneaded it in his hands to form a huge pipe. Then he smoked the pipe, sending smoke out over all the people gathered there. He told them that the stone was their flesh, and that they should make pipes from it. All the tribes were to share this place, and no weapons were ever to be used there. The Great Spirit talked until he had finished smoking, then dissolved into a cloud of smoke. From then on, when the people smoked their sacred pipes at important ceremonies, bringing the smoke into their bodies and then watching it float up into the sky, they felt closer to the spirits who received their offering.

At Pipestone National Monument, near the western edge of Minnesota, Native Americans have been mining the soft, red stone for hundreds of years. This spot is one of the most important places in Native-American culture because only stone dug from this quarry is used to make sacred peace pipes. In the mid-1800s the painter George Catlin visited forty tribes spread over thousands of miles and never saw a pipe that was not made from this stone. Today, Native Americans still dig up the red pipestone and carve it into pipes and jewelry.

Blue Mounds State Park includes a sharp cliff that appears seemingly out of nowhere. The Santee Sioux once hunted buffalo by driving them over the edge. A small herd of buffalo lives in the park today. With miles of trails meandering through more than 2,000 acres, the park is a good place to explore the prairie.

The quartzite rock found in Blue Mounds State Park was formed from the bottom of an ancient sea.

TEN LARGEST CITIES

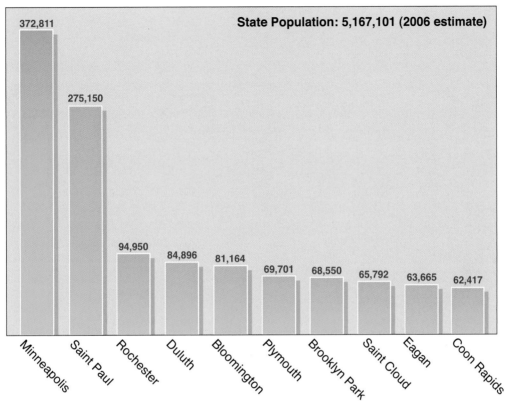

State Population: 5,167,101 (2006 estimate)

City	Population
Minneapolis	372,811
Saint Paul	275,150
Rochester	94,950
Duluth	84,896
Bloomington	81,164
Plymouth	69,701
Brooklyn Park	68,550
Saint Cloud	65,792
Eagan	63,665
Coon Rapids	62,417

CENTRAL LAKES

Farther north is Minnesota's central lake country. The popular tourist towns of Brainerd and Detroit Lakes each have more than four hundred lakes within 25 miles. In addition to its hundreds of nearby lakes, Alexandria contains the Kensington Runestone Museum, which displays a 202-pound rock covered with carvings. Some believe this runestone was left by Vikings who traveled from Norway in 1362. Norwegians probably did not come that early, but many did arrive later. The Heritage Hjemkomst Interpretive Center in Moorhead has exhibits about the region's Scandinavian immigrants. The museum houses a 76-foot replica of a Viking ship named the *Hjemkomst*, which actually sailed to Norway.

GATHERING WILD RICE

Besides large, deep lakes, Minnesota also has shallow lakes that cover about 65,000 acres in the state's north-central and northwest areas. These "rice lakes" are perfect for thick stands of wild rice to grow. The Ojibwe are the only ones allowed to gather wild rice on their reservations' lakes. However, on nonreservation lakes, people can buy a rice-picking license for $25 per person from the Minnesota Department of Natural Resources. This is similar to buying a license to hunt or to fish. However, there's no limit to how much rice any one person can gather. The total wild rice harvest for 2006 was estimated at about 500,000 pounds.

Some people gather wild rice as an early fall family activity, using canoes just as the Ojibwe do. It's hard work pushing the canoe through the thick reeds that contain the wild rice grains. One person uses a long pole to move the canoe forward; the other person strips the grains into the canoe. At the end of the day they'll have enough wild rice to use in soups and other dishes all winter long. Any grains that fall into the water are left for ducks to feast on.

Sprawling Mille Lacs Lake in central Minnesota hosts thousands of vacationers in summer and ice fishers in winter. The excellent Mille Lacs Indian Museum offers exhibits showing how the Ojibwe hunted, fished, collected maple sap, and gathered wild rice two hundred years ago, as well as displays about contemporary Ojibwe life.

Paul Bunyan and his ox Babe can be found in several Minnesota cities.

Another popular place is the source of the Mississippi River at Itasca State Park. Visitors like to wade across the mighty river where it begins, as a shallow, 20-foot-wide stream. Thirty miles northeast is Bemidji, best known for its roadside statues of the legendary lumberjack Paul Bunyan and Babe the blue ox. Other towns also feature statues of Paul Bunyan—Brainerd's even talks—but Bemidji's is the oldest, erected in 1937.

UP NORTH

The Iron Range in northeastern Minnesota offers several places to see where the giant mines turned hills and forests into gaping canyons. The Hull Rust Mine, near Hibbing, is 3 miles long and 2 miles wide. According to one visitor, "It looks like a reddish, rusty Grand Canyon." At the Ironworld Discovery Center, in Chisholm, a museum shows how ore was dug and tells the story of the immigrants who worked the mines. Trolleys take visitors around a once-bustling mine site.

In north-central Minnesota the lakes thin out, and bogs and marshes become plentiful. This region is inhabited mostly by insects.

PLACES TO SEE

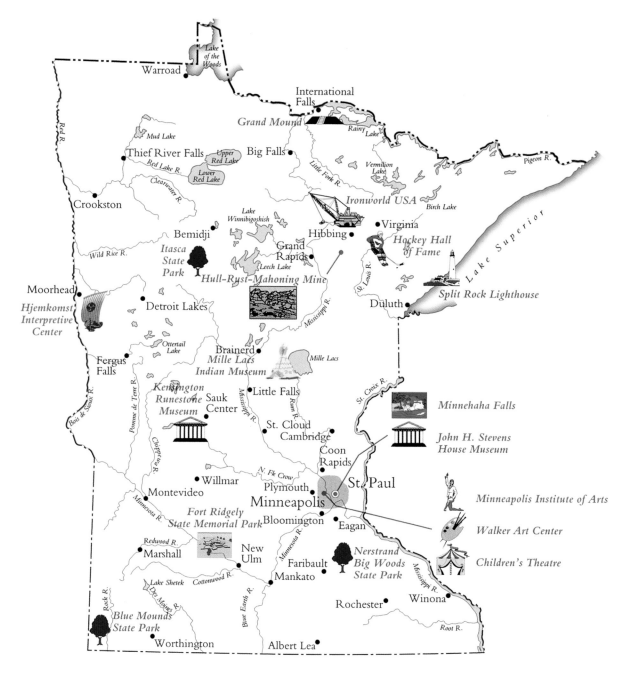

Warroad

Lake of the Woods

International Falls

Grand Mound

Rainy Lake

Red R.

Mud Lake

Thief River Falls

Upper Red Lake

Big Falls

Little Fork R.

Vermilion Lake

Pigeon R.

Red Lake R.

Lower Red Lake

Clearwater R.

Ironworld USA

Birch Lake

Crookston

Lake Winnibigoshish

Bemidji

Itasca State Park

Wild Rice R.

Hibbing

Grand Rapids

Virginia

Hockey Hall of Fame

Lake Superior

Leech Lake

Hull-Rust-Mahoning Mine

St. Louis R.

Split Rock Lighthouse

Moorhead

Hjemkomst Interpretive Center

Detroit Lakes

Mississippi R.

Duluth

Ottertail Lake

Brainerd
Mille Lacs
Indian Museum

Mille Lacs

Fergus Falls

Pomme de Terre R.

Kensington Runestone Museum

Sauk Center

Little Falls

Rum R.

St. Croix R.

Minnehaha Falls

Mississippi R.

St. Cloud

Cambridge

John H. Stevens House Museum

Chippewa R.

Coon Rapids

N. Fk Crow

Willmar

Plymouth

St. Paul

Minneapolis Institute of Arts

Montevideo

Minneapolis

Minnesota R.

Fort Ridgely State Memorial Park

Bloomington

Eagan

Walker Art Center

Redwood R.

Marshall

New Ulm

Faribault

Mankato

Nerstrand Big Woods State Park

Children's Theatre

Mississippi R.

Lake Shetek

Cottonwood R.

Blue Earth R.

Winona

Rock R.

Des Moines R.

Blue Mounds State Park

Rochester

Root R.

Worthington

Albert Lea

Koochiching County has so few people that as recently as the late 1990s, it offered free land to anyone willing to move there. As of 2005 the county had lost 3 percent of its people. At the northern tip of the state is the immense Lake of the Woods. Ninety miles long, it contains 14,000 islands and endless spots for fishing and ice fishing.

The Arrowhead region of northeastern Minnesota is filled with thousands of lovely lakes that make it one of the nation's best canoeing areas. For a classic Minnesota vacation, many Twin Cities residents hop in the car and head north on Interstate 35. Before long the cities and suburbs thin out, giving way to farmland. Then lakes and thick forests appear. After about three hours the road climbs to the top of a large hill. Spread out below is the city of Duluth, wrapped around a shimmering harbor at the tip of Lake Superior. In the harbor area kids can have fun at Canal Park, the Great Lakes Aquarium, and the Great Lakes Zoo. Because cool breezes blow off Lake Superior in the summer, Duluth is known as the air-conditioned city.

Past Duluth the road follows the lake northeastward along the North Shore of Lake Superior. At times the road rises and hugs a rocky cliff, and the view of the cool blue water is breathtaking. Frothing rivers cut through the rocks to splash into Lake Superior, the largest freshwater lake in the world. For a break in the drive, travelers can get out and run among the rocks and trees or pick wild raspberries along the lake's rugged, rocky shore.

Driving straight north, travelers once again are in the woods and can find crystal-clear lakes for canoeing. They might be joined on the lake by a pair of loons bobbing nearby. As Chester Anderson wrote in *Growing Up in Minnesota*, "It's worth the trip, especially for kids, to hear the loony laughter. First the loon laughs. A kid will laugh back, naturally, and the loon will reply, joining in an endless exchanging of echoing fun. Minnesota is a good place in which to grow up."

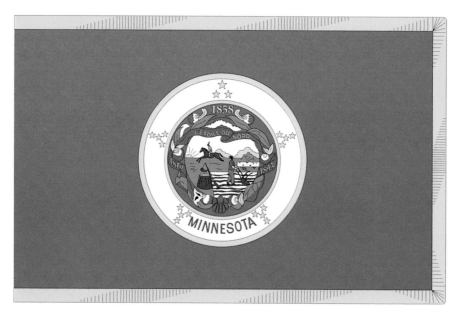

THE FLAG: The state flag is deep blue with a gold fringe. In the center is the state seal surrounded by a wreath of lady's slippers, the state flower. Around the wreath is a ring of nineteen stars, representing the fact that Minnesota was the nineteenth state admitted to the Union after the thirteen original states. The flag was adopted in 1957.

THE SEAL: The state seal, adopted in 1861, shows a farmer plowing a field by hand near a waterfall on the Mississippi River. His ax, gun, and powder horn rest on a nearby stump, and he is watching a Native American on horseback riding by. Above the farmer and Native American is a scroll with the state motto in French, L'Etoile du Nord (The Star of the North). Surrounding this scene is a border that reads "The Great Seal of the State of Minnesota, 1858."

State Survey

Statehood: May 11, 1858

Origin of Name: From a Santee Sioux term for "sky-tinted water"

Nickname: North Star State, Land of 10,000 Lakes, The Gopher State

Capital: St. Paul

Motto: *L'Etoile du Nord* ("The Star of the North")

Bird: Common loon

Fish: Walleye pike

Flower: Pink and white lady's slipper

Tree: Norway pine

Gem: Lake Superior agate

Fruit: Honeycrisp apple

Grain: Wild rice

Mushroom: Morel

Common loon

Lady's slipper

HAIL! MINNESOTA

Truman Rickard, who graduated from the University of Minnesota in 1904, wrote the music and this verse of "Hail! Minnesota," which was the school song until it was adopted as the official state song in 1945.

By Truman E. Rickard

Min-ne-so-ta, hail to thee! Hail to thee, our col-lege dear!— Thy—

light shall ev-er be A— bea-con bright and clear. Thy—

sons and daugh-ters true Will pro-claim thee near and far.— They will

guard thy fame and a-dore thy name; Thou shalt be their North-ern Star.

GEOGRAPHY

Highest Point: 2,301 feet above sea level, at Eagle Mountain in Cook County

Lowest Point: 602 feet above sea level, along Lake Superior

Area: 86,943 square miles

Greatest Distance North to South: 411 miles

Greatest Distance East to West: 357 miles

Bordering States: Wisconsin to the east, Iowa to the south, North Dakota and South Dakota to the west, and the Canadian provinces of Manitoba and Ontario to the north

Hottest Recorded Temperature: 114° F at Beardsley on July 29, 1917, and at Moorhead on July 6, 1936

Coldest Recorded Temperature: –60° F at Tower on February 2, 1996

Average Annual Precipitation: 26 inches

Major Rivers: Blue Earth, Cannon, Crow Wing, Little Fork, Middle, Minnesota, Mississippi, Pomme de Terre, Rapid, Red, Red Lake, Redwood, St. Croix, St. Louis, Thief, Wild Rice

Major Lakes: Big Sandy, Bowstring, Gull, Kabetogama, Lake of the Woods, Leech, Lower Red, Mille Lacs, Minnetonka, Minnewaska, Osakis, Otter Tail, Pelican, Pepin, Pokegama, Superior, Upper Red, Vermilion, Winnibigoshish

Trees: Ash, aspen, balsam, beech, birch, black walnut, elm, fir, maple, oak, pine, poplar, spruce

Wild Plants: Aster, bird's-foot violet, blazing star, bulrush, golden-rod, honeysuckle, kitten tails, lady's slipper, prairie phlox, sweet fern thimbleberry, trailing arbutus, water lily, wintergreen

Mammals: Badger, beaver, black bear, bobcat, fox, gopher, gray wolf, moose, opossum, otter, porcupine, raccoon, skunk, squirrel, white-tailed deer

Birds: Bald eagle, blackbird, duck, loon, meadowlark, owl, peregrine falcon, pheasant, robin, sparrow, woodpecker, wren

Fish: Bass, carp, catfish, lake herring, muskellunge, northern pike, smelt, trout, walleye pike, whitefish, yellow perch

Amphibians: Blanding's turtle, wood turtle

Endangered Animals: Assiniboia skipper, Baird's sparrow, burrowing owl, chestnut-collared longspur, Henslow's sparrow, Karner blue butterfly, king rail, massasauga, northern cricket frog, piping plover, Sprague's pipit, Uhler's arctic butterfly, uncas skipper

Burrowing owls

Endangered Plants: Alpine milk vetch, ball cactus, bog adder's-mouth, dwarf trout lily, eared false foxglove, floating marsh marigold, hairy lip-fern, handsome sedge, Indian ricegrass, knotty pearlwort, narrow-leaved milkweed, nodding saxifrage, Norwegian whitlow-grass, pale moonwort, purple crowberry, round-stemmed false foxglove, sweet-smelling Indian-plantain, Virginia bartonia, wild quinine, Wolf's spike rush

TIME LINE

Minnesota History

1500s Santee Sioux live in what becomes northern Minnesota.

1600s Ojibwe Indians migrate to northern Minnesota from Canada.

1600 French traders Pierre Radisson and Médard Chouart explore the Minnesota shores of Lake Superior.

1679 Daniel Greysolon, Sieur du Lhut, explores northeastern Minnesota and claims the region for France.

1680 Father Louis Hennepin discovers St. Anthony Falls on the site of present-day Minneapolis.

1689 The French build a trading post named St. Antoine, the first in the region, near Lake Pepin.

1732 Pierre Gaultier de Varennes, Sieur de La Vérendrye, builds the first French fort in Minnesota on the shores of Lake of the Woods.

1762 France cedes land in Minnesota west of the Mississippi River to Spain.

1763 France cedes land in Minnesota east of the Mississippi River to Britain as part of the treaty ending the French and Indian War.

1783 The United States gains the part of Minnesota east of the Mississippi as a result of its victory in the American Revolution.

1803 The United States gains the rest of Minnesota as part of the Louisiana Purchase.

1820 Construction begins on Fort St. Anthony at the site where the Mississippi and Minnesota rivers join; it is renamed Fort Snelling in 1825.

1832 Henry Schoolcraft discovers the source of the Mississippi River at Lake Itasca in north-central Minnesota.

1837 Santee Sioux and Ojibwe Indians cede a large portion of their territory in east-central Minnesota to the United States.

1849 The Minnesota Territory is created.

1851 Santee Sioux Indians sign a treaty giving up their remaining territory in southern Minnesota.

1858 Minnesota becomes the thirty-second state.

1862 Santee Sioux Indians, angry about land treaties and U.S. Indian policies, launch an uprising that kills about five hundred settlers.

1889 The physician William Mayo and his sons begin operating a hospital in Rochester.

1892 The first shipments of iron ore leave the Mesabi Range.

1918 Forest fires destroy about 2,000 square miles of forest in northeastern Minnesota and kill hundreds of people.

1930 Floyd Olson of the Farmer-Labor Party is elected governor, the first person from a third party elected governor of any state.

1944 The Farmer-Labor Party merges with the Democratic Party, giving the Democrats strong support among rural Minnesotans.

1959 The opening of the St. Lawrence Seaway makes Duluth the westernmost port connected to the Atlantic Ocean.

1969 Minnesotan Warren Burger is appointed chief justice of the U.S. Supreme Court.

1992 The state pioneers a health-insurance program to help the poor and unemployed; Mall of America opens.

1993 Almost half of Minnesota's counties are declared disaster areas because of the severe flooding of the Mississippi River.

1994 Sharon Sayles Belton becomes the first African-American mayor of Minneapolis as well as the first female mayor of that city.

1998 Jesse Ventura, a former wrestler, is elected governor.

2002 Democratic U.S. senator Paul Wellstone, his wife, and their daughter die in a plane crash a few weeks before the November election in which he was running; Republican Tim Pawlenty is elected governor.

2004 Minneapolis's first light rail, the Hiawatha Line, opens.

2006 Minneapolis experiences an explosion of the arts; Pawlenty is reelected as governor; Keith Ellison, an African-American Muslim, becomes the first person of that religion to be elected to the U.S. Congress.

2007 Ellison uses the Qur'an during the unofficial swearing-in to the House of Representatives.

2008 Minnesota celebrates its sesquicentennial (150 years) of statehood; St. Paul hosts the Republican National Convention.

ECONOMY

Agricultural Products: Beef, butter, cheese, corn, milk, peas, pork, potatoes, poultry, rye, soybeans, sugar beets, wheat

Manufactured Products: Canned foods, cereals, chemicals, computers and computer equipment, farm and construction machinery, lumber products, paper products, printed materials, scientific and medical instruments

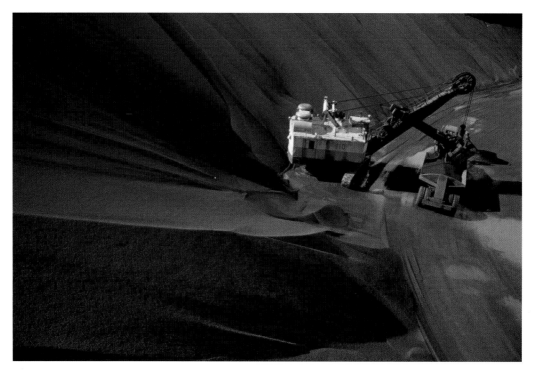

Iron ore

Natural Resources: Forests, granite, gravel, iron ore, limestone, sandstone, taconite

Business and Trade: Banking, communications, data processing, health care, insurance, transportation, wholesale and retail sales

CALENDAR OF CELEBRATIONS

Burns Night Each January 24 the town of Mapleton joins people of Scottish descent throughout the world in celebrating the birthday of the Scottish poet Robert Burns. The celebration includes Scottish songs and dances, bagpipe music, and traditional Scottish foods.

Cabin Fever Days At the end of January the people of Cannon Falls treat their winter "cabin fever" with a celebration featuring sled-dog races, ski races, and a parade of horse-drawn sleighs.

St. Paul Winter Carnival From late January into early February, St. Paul holds the nation's oldest and largest winter festival, which started in 1886. This ten-day event now features more than one hundred activities, including two parades, cultural celebrations, ice-and snow-sculpting competitions, and the crowning of a royal court.

St. Paul Winter Carnival

Ice Box Days International Falls celebrates its famously frigid winters each January with various winter events. Included are the Freeze Yer Gizzard Blizzard 10K race and the Frostbite Falls Ski Classic. Visitors are advised to bring plenty of warm clothes.

Fasching Held on the day before the beginning of Lent (usually in February), this celebration in New Ulm is the traditional German equivalent of Mardi Gras. The festival includes music, costume contests, German food, and arts and crafts.

St. Urho's Day Close to March 16 the town of Finland holds a four-day celebration in honor of the Finnish saint who supposedly drove the grasshoppers out of Finland. The celebration includes a parade, music, dancing, and food.

Annual Eagle Watch Bird-watchers from around the United States gather in Stillwater each March to view the annual migration of bald eagles along the St. Croix River.

Mai Feiertag On the first Sunday in May people in Montrose celebrate spring in keeping with their German heritage. This festival features a maypole raising—the erecting of a tall pole festooned with long, colorful ribbons, which people dance around, accompanied by traditional German music.

Ripplin-River Daze Held in Zumbro Falls in June, this festival features parades, sports competitions, street dancing, fireworks, an exhibit of artifacts showcasing the town's founding in the 1890s, and lots of food.

Great American Think-Off Each June, New York Mills hosts this national philosophy competition geared toward the everyday person rather than academic scholars. Finalists participate in a live philosophical debate, and the audience chooses the winner.

Vikingland Band Festival The finest high school marching bands in the Midwest gather in Alexandria each June to stage a dazzling parade competition. This event typically draws more than 2,000 performers and 30,000 spectators.

Timber Days In June the town of Cook celebrates its lumber industry with a festival featuring lumberjack contests, craft demonstrations, art, food, and entertainment. Also included are a carnival and parade.

Bean Hole Days Each July the people of Pequot Lakes cook 150 gallons of Boston baked beans over fires in pits in the ground. This festival is held in honor of the New England origin of the town's name (after the Pequot Indians of Connecticut). The event also features other foods and an arts and crafts fair.

Taste of Minnesota From the end of June until the Fourth of July, one of Minnesota's great food festivals takes place on Harriet Island in the Mississippi River, between Minneapolis and St. Paul. With fireworks each night and three stages with free entertainment, including *American Idol* winners, festivalgoers keep busy between bites of food.

Minneapolis Aquatennial Since 1939 Minneapolis has hosted this water-based event that highlights its many lakes. Each July this ten-day celebration features sailing regattas on Lake Calhoun, a triathlon at Lake Nokomis, and waterskiing shows and speedboat races on the Mississippi River. Other events include parades, fireworks, and the coronation of the Queen of the Lakes.

Wrong Days In July the town of Wright celebrates its opposite—wrong—with dances, amateur talent contests, a crafts fair, sports competitions, a parade, and a smorgasbord of good food.

Upper Sioux Wacipi The Santee Sioux Indian ceremony "wacipi" honors tribal elders, youth, and departed loved ones. Held in July at the Upper Sioux Agency State Park near Granite Falls, this event includes people in ceremonial dress, drumming, dancing, and singing.

Great River Shakespeare Festival Held in July and August in Winona, this festival showcases plays by William Shakespeare as well as music from some of America's new performers and an art exhibition.

Stiftungsfest Held each August in Norwood Young America, this celebration, which means "Founder's Festival" in German, features singing, dancing, crafts, sports contests, food, and rides. First held in 1861, this festival is Minnesota's oldest festival.

Itasca Pioneer Farmers Show Held at Lake Itasca in August, this event features parades, old-time tractor pulls, lumber-sawing contests, demonstrations of farm activities, logging displays, and traditional music.

Minnesota State Fair Held annually in St. Paul from the end of August into September, this is one of the nation's largest and best-attended agricultural fairs. More than 1.5 million visitors come to see exhibits of fine arts, crafts, and much more. The livestock competitions are a favorite.

Big Island Rendezvous and Festival Held in early October in Albert Lea, this living-history reenactment celebrates life in America during the fur-trading years. More than one thousand participants in period dress live in about 250 tents. Visitors can eat early American foods and watch how early Americans did blacksmithing and made wood products, pottery, and candles.

Festival of Lights Between the end of November and beginning of January, Canal Park in Duluth lights up the holiday season with Christmas parades, special events, and colorful holiday displays.

STATE STARS

Charles Bender (1883–1954), a member of the Baseball Hall of Fame, was born on the White Earth Indian Reservation, near Brainerd. The son of a German-American father and an Ojibwe mother, Bender played baseball and football at the Carlisle Indian School in Pennsylvania. He signed with the Philadelphia Athletics in 1903 and played in several World Series. In 1913 he became the first pitcher to win six World Series games. After retiring, he worked as a college and major-league coach.

Patty Berg (1918–2006), one of the greatest
female golfers ever, was born in Minneapolis. Berg began playing amateur golf in her
teens and gained national recognition by age
seventeen. She turned professional in 1940
and won more than eighty tournaments,
including a record fifteen major championships. A founder of the U.S. Ladies' Professional Golfers' Association, Berg also served
as its first president. She was elected to the
Golfing Hall of Fame in 1974.

Patty Berg

Harry A. Blackmun (1908–1999) was an associate justice of the U.S.
Supreme Court. Although born in Illinois, Blackmun grew up in Minneapolis and St. Paul. After earning a law degree at Harvard in 1932, he
returned to Minnesota to practice law. In 1959 he was appointed to the
U.S. Court of Appeals, and in 1970 he was appointed to the U.S.
Supreme Court. In 1973 Blackmun wrote the majority opinion in *Roe
v. Wade*, the landmark decision that gave women the right to choose to
have abortions. Blackmun retired from the Court in 1994.

Robert Bly (1926–   ), a poet and lecturer, was born in Madison. After
serving in the navy in World War II, Bly studied literature and earned a
degree from Harvard University in 1950. He has spent his life writing,
lecturing, and teaching. In the 1960s he became a well-known activist
protesting the Vietnam War. In 1990 Bly published a book called *Iron
John: A Book About Men*, which became a best seller and helped launch
a movement among men to rediscover their masculinity.

Warren E. Burger (1907–1995), a chief justice of the U.S. Supreme Court, was born in St. Paul. Burger began practicing law in 1931 and became involved in the civil rights movement in the 1940s. In 1953 he was appointed assistant attorney general in charge of civil rights. He was named chief justice of the Supreme Court in 1969. While on the Court Burger worked hard to improve the efficiency of the entire judicial system. He retired in 1986.

Joel (1954–   ) and **Ethan** (1957–   ) **Coen** were born in St. Louis Park. As boys they were obsessed with movies and even made their own. As adults they have made films that have won awards for screenwriting, acting, and directing. Probably their most famous film is *Fargo*, which showcases the Coens' trademark dark humor. In it they poked fun at "Minnesota Nice" and the way Minnesotans talk. The film's dialogue earned the Coens an Academy Award for Best Original Screenplay in 1997.

William O. Douglas (1898–1980), born in Maine, Minnesota, served as an associate justice of the U.S. Supreme Court from 1939 to 1975—the longest any individual has served on the Court. After graduating from Columbia University Law School in 1925, Douglas worked briefly as a corporate lawyer and then taught law. In 1939 President Franklin Roosevelt appointed him to the U.S. Supreme Court. Only forty years old at the time, Douglas was the second-youngest justice in the Court's history. During his many years on the Court, Douglas became known for his outspoken defense of civil liberties, especially freedom of speech and of the press.

Bob Dylan (1941–   ) was born Robert
Zimmerman in Duluth. In the 1960s
he started a new sound in music—folk
songs sung to a rock-and-roll beat. He
is best known for songs protesting the
Vietnam War and supporting civil
rights, including "The Times They Are
A-Changin'," "Blowin' in the Wind,"
and "Masters of War." In 1998 he won
three Grammy Awards for the brood-
ing, gloomy "Time Out of Mind."
Three years later his song "Things
Have Changed" won the Academy
Award for Best Song.

Bob Dylan

Richard G. Eberhart (1904–2005), a well-known poet, was born in
Austin. The author of several respected collections of poetry, including
A Bravery of Earth and *Burr Oaks*, Eberhart also taught literature at
several colleges, including the University of Washington and Dartmouth
College. Eberhart won a number of prestigious awards, including the
Pulitzer Prize for Poetry in 1966. Many of his poems reflect a love for
nature that he gained as a young boy living in rural Minnesota.

Wanda Gág (1893–1946), an artist and writer born in New Ulm,
was best known for her brilliant children's book *Millions of Cats*,
which was published in 1928. Her other children's books include
Snippy and Snappy and *Nothing-at-All*. In 1940 she published
Growing Pains, a description of her childhood.

Judy Garland (1922–1969), a popular singer and actor, was born Frances Gumm in Grand Rapids. The daughter of entertainers, Garland first appeared on stage at age three. She later toured the United States with her sisters in a musical act. Garland made her first film in 1936 and soon became a well-known child star. Her role as Dorothy in *The Wizard of Oz* made her one of the most famous stars in Hollywood.

Judy Garland

J. Paul Getty (1892–1976), born in Minneapolis, was reportedly the wealthiest man in the world at the time of his death. Getty began buying and selling oil leases in Oklahoma in 1913 with the help of his father, an oil millionaire. A gifted entrepreneur, the younger Getty earned his first million dollars by age twenty-four. During the 1920s he gained control of several oil companies and built a financial empire. He was a billionaire by the mid-1950s. The J. Paul Getty Museum in Los Angeles, California, founded by Getty in 1953, displays many of the art objects he collected during his lifetime.

Hubert H. Humphrey (1911–1978), a vice president of the United States, was born in Wallace, South Dakota, but spent much of his adult life in Minnesota. Humphrey became involved in politics in 1944, when he served as the Minnesota campaign manager for Franklin Roosevelt. He launched his own political career in 1945, when he was elected mayor of Minneapolis. In 1948 Humphrey was elected to the U.S. Senate. He served for sixteen years, gaining a reputation as an effective leader and a strong supporter of liberal ideas. Elected vice president under Lyndon Johnson in 1964, Humphrey worked on civil rights and antipoverty programs. He ran for president in 1968 but was narrowly defeated by Richard Nixon.

Jessica Lange (1949–   ), an award-winning actor, was born in Cloquet. She first pursued a career in art and then began studying acting while living in New York. Her first movie was a remake of the classic movie *King Kong*. Lange went on to become one of the most respected actors in Hollywood. She won the Oscar for Best Supporting Actress in 1982 for her role in *Tootsie* and the Oscar for Best Actress in 1994 for her performance in *Blue Sky*. In recent years Lange has returned to Minnesota to live.

Charles Lindbergh (1902–1974), a famous aviator, was born in Detroit, Michigan, but spent his childhood in Little Falls. Lindbergh learned to fly at age twenty and started flying a mail route between Chicago and St. Louis in 1926. In 1927, in a plane called the *Spirit of St. Louis*, he became the first person to fly solo across the Atlantic Ocean. The successful flight made Lindbergh a world-famous hero. Tragedy struck Lindbergh and his wife in 1932, when their infant son was kidnapped and murdered.

John Madden (1936–   ), a sports commentator and former football coach, was born in Austin. Involved in sports throughout his school years, Madden was drafted by the Philadelphia Eagles in 1959, but a leg injury ended his professional career before it even began. Unable to play, he turned to coaching. He coached the Oakland Raiders for ten years, leading them to a Super Bowl championship in 1977. In 1979 Madden began teaching, acting in commercials, and broadcasting sports commentaries on radio and television. He has won several Emmy Awards as a sports analyst and commentator. In 2006 he was elected as a coach to the Pro Football Hall of Fame.

Roger Maris (1934–1985), a baseball outfielder, was born in Hibbing. Maris played football and baseball in high school and began playing minor-league baseball in 1953. In 1957 he entered the major leagues, playing for the Cleveland Indians, Kansas City Athletics, and New York Yankees. In 1961, while with the Yankees, Maris made baseball history by hitting sixty-one home runs in a single season, a record that stood until 1998.

Roger Maris

Eugene McCarthy (1916–2005), a U.S. senator and presidential candidate, was born in Watkins. After serving in World War II, McCarthy taught in Minnesota at St. John's University and at St. Thomas College. He ran successfully for the U.S. House of Representatives in 1948 and served until 1958, when he was elected to the U.S. Senate. An outspoken critic of the Vietnam War, McCarthy successfully challenged President Lyndon Johnson in early 1968 Democratic primaries for the presidential election. Although he was not chosen as the Democratic presidential candidate, he continued to speak out against the war. McCarthy retired from the Senate in 1970.

Walter Mondale (1928–   ), a vice president of the United States, was born in Ceylon. Trained as a lawyer, he became active in politics in college, when he worked on Hubert Humphrey's first campaign for the U.S. Senate. In 1965 Mondale was appointed to Humphrey's seat when the senator became vice president. Elected to the Senate on his own in 1966, he won reelection in 1972. In 1976 he ran successfully for vice president under President Jimmy Carter. While in office, Mondale favored liberal policies and was a strong supporter of civil rights and education reform. In 1984 he ran unsuccessfully for the presidency against Ronald Reagan.

Prince (1958–   ), a popular musician, was named Prince Rogers Nelson at birth in Minneapolis. As a teenager he produced an album for which he wrote all the music, sang all the songs, and played all the instruments. Prince's music became known as the "Minneapolis Sound." His 1982 hit "1999" sold three million copies. Two years later he starred in and wrote the music for the film *Purple Rain*. Its soundtrack sold more than 11 million copies. In 1993 Prince changed his name to a symbol and was called the Artist Formerly Known as Prince. Finally, in 2000 he returned to using "Prince" as his name.

Winona Ryder (1971–   ), a highly respected actor, was born Winona Horowitz and named after her birthplace of Winona, Minnesota. Ryder had an unconventional childhood, moving with her non-conformist, intellectual parents to a communal farm in California when she was about ten. She began taking acting classes at age thirteen and found that she loved playing different characters. Noticed by a talent scout, she got her first movie role while she was in the eighth grade. Ryder has appeared in many movies, including *The Age of Innocence* and *The Crucible*.

Winona Ryder

Harrison E. Salisbury (1908–1993), a well-known author and journalist, was born in Minneapolis. Although he originally planned to be a chemist, he discovered his talent for journalism while reporting for his college newspaper. Salisbury began working for the United Press in 1930 and moved to the agency's London office in 1943. A few years later he joined *The New York Times* and became a well-known foreign correspondent. Salisbury returned to New York in 1954 and worked as an editor and correspondent for the *Times* for many years, during which he won a number of journalism awards.

Charles Schulz (1922–2000), the cartoonist who created the comic strip *Peanuts* about Charlie Brown, Snoopy, and their friends, was born in Minneapolis. Not a particularly good student, Schulz began drawing cartoons in high school. After serving in World War II, he settled in St. Paul and began drawing a weekly cartoon for a local newspaper. Within a few years *Peanuts* was born, and it soon appeared in newspapers across the country. Schulz published a number of collections of the comic strip.

Richard W. Sears (1863–1914) was a merchant who founded one of the nation's most successful mail-order businesses. Born in Stewartville, Sears worked for a railroad for a number of years. He began selling watches through the mail in 1886. He soon hired an assistant, Alvah Roebuck, and moved the business to Chicago. The business expanded quickly, and Sears took on Roebuck as a partner. The company eventually became known as Sears, Roebuck and Company. By 1894 the company's mail-order catalog had more than five hundred pages of items for sale.

Elaine Stately (1937–1988), a Native-American activist, was born on the White Earth Indian Reservation in west-central Minnesota. An Ojibwe, Stately was one of the founders of the American Indian Movement, an Indian civil rights group established in 1972. She also started a Native-American Olympics.

DeWitt Wallace (1889–1981), the founder of *Reader's Digest* magazine, was born in St. Paul. After attending college, Wallace worked for several years as a book salesman in St. Paul. While selling books, he got the idea of publishing a magazine that contained articles gathered from other magazines. He brought his idea to life in 1920 when he began publishing *Reader's Digest*. Wallace's magazine went on to become one of the most popular in the United States.

Dave Winfield (1951–   ), an all-star baseball player, was born in St. Paul. In high school Winfield excelled in both baseball and basketball, but he focused on baseball in college. He began his professional baseball career in 1973, when he joined the San Diego Padres. He played for the Padres until 1980 and established himself as one of the stars of the team. In 1980 Winfield signed with the New York Yankees for a record-breaking salary of $20 million paid over ten years. Winfield later played for the California Angels and the Toronto Blue Jays before ending his career with the Minnesota Twins in 1993. In 2001 he was elected to the Baseball Hall of Fame.

TOUR THE STATE

Boundary Waters Canoe Area Wilderness (Ely) A unique preserve of forest and water, the Boundary Waters is the greatest wilderness canoeing and fishing area in the world. More than one thousand lakes and streams lie within this vast forested area, offering canoeists solitude and unspoiled beauty.

Split Rock Lighthouse (Two Harbors) Located on the shores of Lake Superior, this lighthouse has warned ships away from a dangerous, rocky coast since 1910. One of Minnesota's best-known landmarks, it offers a glimpse of life in a remote and spectacular setting. In addition to touring the lighthouse, you can visit a history center that features exhibits and a film.

Fort Snelling (St. Paul) This restored stone military post was built between 1820 and 1825. It features exhibits of artifacts and demonstrations showing what life was like in Minnesota in the 1820s.

Sibley House (Mendota) Built in 1836, this historic stone building was the home of Henry H. Sibley, a prominent fur trader and Minnesota's first state governor. Exhibits and guided tours reveal information about Sibley and his family, the fur trade, and the history of the Native Americans of the region.

Forest History Center (Grand Rapids) A re-creation of a turn-of-the-century logging camp, the center features exhibits, logging demonstrations, forest trails, and lectures about forest resource conservation.

Forest History Center

Mall of America (Bloomington) The largest shopping mall in the United States, the enormous Mall of America includes more than five hundred stores, fourteen movie theaters, about sixty restaurants, an indoor amusement park complete with a roller coaster, and an underground aquarium.

Mille Lacs Indian Museum (Onamia) Exhibits at this museum trace the history of the Mille Lacs band of Ojibwe Indians. The museum also features a handmade birchbark canoe, mannequins made from body casts of live tribal members in the 1970s, craft demonstrations, and films about modern Ojibwe life.

Murphy's Landing (Shakopee) This re-creation of an 1890s Minnesota pioneer village features replicas of farms, a fur trader's cabin, a small Native American village, and other period buildings.

Pipestone National Monument (Pipestone) This monument preserves land held sacred by many Native American tribes. The Indians used the soft red stone, to make peace pipes and other objects. An interpretive center tells about the quarry's history and geology and displays Indian crafts.

Charles A. Lindbergh State Park (Little Falls) This park is built around the childhood home of the famous aviator. Built in 1906, the house contains some original Lindbergh family possessions. The park also includes a history center with exhibits about Lindbergh and the area.

Minnesota History Center (St. Paul) The center houses many exhibits about Minnesota history—everything from a 24-ton boxcar to a canoe used for fur trading. Visitors can watch presentations by costumed characters representing various periods in the state's history.

St. Anthony Falls Historic District (Minneapolis) Visitors to this historic district can view the only waterfall on the Mississippi River as well as the ruins of a flour-milling district that was once the largest in the world. A self-guided trail running for 2 miles along the Minneapolis riverfront has signs describing the history of the Native Americans and the early settlers of the riverfront area.

Mill City Museum (Minneapolis) A study in contrasts, this modern, glass-enclosed museum was built within the ruins of one of the Washburn Crosby flour mills. Visitors can ride the eight-story Flour Tower elevator, bake and eat bread in the Baking Lab, and learn how St. Anthony Falls and the Mississippi River made flour milling possible in the Water Lab.

Jeffers Petroglyphs (Comfrey) Amid acres of prairie grasses are islands of rock where ancient people made carvings, known as petroglyphs, of people and animals. Some estimated to be five thousand years old, the carvings record important events and ceremonies. A visitor's center and self-guided trails focus on the history of the petroglyphs and the ecological changes that have occurred at the site over the last five thousand years.

Grand Portage National Monument (Grand Portage) Located at the northeastern tip of Minnesota, the monument includes a restored fur-trading post originally built by the North West Company. Costumed guides take visitors back to the days of the French fur traders and explorers. Nearby Grand Portage State Park offers scenic views of a spectacular 200-foot waterfall, the highest in Minnesota.

Minnesota Museum of Mining (Chisholm) The museum has a restored mining village and other exhibits that present the history of mining in the state.

Oliver H. Kelley Farm and Interpretive Center (Elk River) This farm museum was the birthplace of the National Grange, a farm organization founded in 1867 that worked to improve the lives of farmers. The center features actual farm activities and demonstrations of domestic crafts, such as quilting, basket making, and blacksmithing.

Hull Rust Mine (Hibbing) Known as the Grand Canyon of Minnesota, this is the largest open-pit mine in the world. The enormous iron mine is 3 miles long, 2 miles wide, and 500 feet deep.

Voyageurs National Park (International Falls) Minnesota's only national park, Voyageurs features thirty lakes and a network of interconnected waterways. Originally part of the "water highway" that carried fur traders throughout the region, the park is a popular place for canoeing and camping.

North Shore Commercial Fishing Museum (Tofte) Housed in a replica of a dark red fish house built by early fishermen in the area, the museum features displays detailing the lives of early settlers and the fishing industry.

International Wolf Center (Ely) This center features not only exhibits on wolf legends and behavior, hands-on activities and interactive exhibits for kids, and various naturalist programs, it also has a live wolf pack that visitors can observe.

International Wolf Center

FUN FACTS

Because of its thousands of lakes, Minnesota has more miles of shoreline than California, Florida, and Hawaii combined.

One of the largest logjams in history occurred on the St. Croix River near Taylors Falls in 1886. It took two hundred men six weeks to break up the jam, which ran for about 2 miles along the river.

From its founding in 1838 until 1841, St. Paul was called Pig's Eye after its first settler, Pierre "Pig's Eye" Parrant.

During the winter of 1888 the people of St. Paul built an ice palace for its winter festival. Until the weather warmed up and melted it, the ice structure was one of the largest buildings in the world, standing fourteen stories high and covering an acre of land.

Minnesota has more miles of bicycle paths along abandoned railroad tracks than any other state. The state's 450 miles of rail-to-trail bikeways wind through woods, farmland, and towns; over streams; and along lakes.

Find Out More

If you'd like to find out more about Minnesota, look in your school library, local public library, bookstores, or video stores. Here are some titles to ask for.

GENERAL STATE BOOKS

Hasdy, Judy L. *Minnesota*. Danbury, CT: Children's Press, 2003.

Kjarum, Roxanne, and Berit Thorkelson. *Only in Minnesota*. Stillwater, MN: Voyageur Press, 2003.

Pohlen, Jerome. *Oddball Minnesota: A Guide to Some Really Strange Places*. Chicago: Chicago Review Press, 2003.

Weinberger, Mark. *Minnesota: Off the Beaten Path*. Guilford, CT: Globe Pequot Press, 2005.

SPECIAL INTEREST BOOKS

Cornell, George L., and Gordon Henry. *Ojibwa* (North American Indians Today). Broomall, PA: Mason Crest Publishing, 2003.

Marsh, Carole. *Minnesota History Projects: 30 Cool Activities, Crafts, Experiments & More for Kids to Do to Learn About Your State*. Decatur, GA: Gallopade International, 2003.

FICTION AND POETRY

Bauer, Marion Dane. *Land of the Buffalo Bones: The Diary of Mary Ann Elizabeth Rodgers, an English Girl in Minnesota*. New York: Scholastic, 2003.

Williams, Julie. *Escaping Tornado Season: A Story in Poems*. New York: HarperTeen, 2004.

AUDIO AND VIDEO SOURCES

Keillor, Garrison. *A Prairie Home Companion (30th Broadcast Season Celebration)*. Cambridge, MA: Rounder Records, 2004. Available in CD and DVD format, running just under 120 minutes.

WEB SITES

Explore Minnesota Tourism
http://www.exploreminnesota.com
Travel and tourism information on attractions, events, and trip ideas.

Minneapolis Star Tribune
http://www.startribune.com
Newspaper articles on all subjects, as well as links to Minnesota-related Web sites.

Minnesota Department of Natural Resources
http://www.dnr.state.mn.us
Information on state parks, trails, lakes, rivers, and wildlife.

Minnesota Historical Society
http://www.mnhs.org
Information on state historic sites, events, and more.

The Official State Web Site
http://www.state.mn.us
Minnesota state government Web site.

Index

Page numbers in **boldface** are illustrations and charts.

ABOUT THE AUTHORS

Martin Schwabacher grew up in Minneapolis, Minnesota. As a boy he enjoyed camping and canoeing and joined the Youth Conservation Corps. Though he has lived in Rhode Island, New York, and Texas, he still considers himself a Minnesotan and returns whenever he can to the north shore of Lake Superior, his favorite vacation spot. He has written and edited many books for young people.

Patricia K. Kummer was born and grew up in Minneapolis, graduated from Burnsville High School in Burnsville, received her B.A. degree in history from the College of St. Catherine in St. Paul, and spent many summers "up north" at her parents' lake home, north of Nisswa. Kummer also has an M.A. degree in history from Marquette University in Milwaukee, Wisconsin. She lives in Lisle, Illinois, with her husband and enjoys spending time with their grown children and young grand-daughters as well as traveling. Some trips take her back to Minnesota to visit family and friends.